The Politics of Ideas

The Politics of Ideas

Intellectual Challenges Facing the American Political Parties

Edited by
John Kenneth White
and
John C. Green

State University of New York Press

Cover photo: Digital Imagery® copyright 2001. PhotoDisc, Inc.

Published by
State University of New York Press, Albany

For information, address State University of New York Press,
90 State Street, Suite 700, Albany, NY 12207

Production by Judith Block
Marketing by Patrick Durocher

Library of Congress Cataloging-in-Publication Data

The politics of ideas : intellectual challenges facing the American political parties /
edited by John Kenneth White, John C. Green.
    p. cm.
Includes bibliographical references and index.
ISBN 0-7914-5043-0 (alk. paper)—ISBN 0-7914-5044-9 (pbk. : alk. paper)
1. Political parties—United States. 2. Ideology—United States. I. White, John Kenneth,
1952–II. Green, John Clifford, 1953–

JK2261.P673 2001
324.273'013—dc21   00-051587

10 9 8 7 6 5 4 3 2 1

To the memory of Everett Carll Ladd
(1937–1999)
Pro debitas plurimis seras gratias

Contents

1

The Politics of Ideas: Introduction

JOHN C. GREEN

Ideas are just one of the many fuels that power American democracy, often competing with group identities, tangible interests, and the influences of organization and strategy. However, the power of ideas is both deeper and broader. It is deeper because ideas ultimately underlie the power of identities, interests, and other influences, and it is broader because ideas have greater and longer-term consequences. Thus, ideas lie at the root of political problems and are central to their resolution, for good or ill. Indeed, it is this capacity for good and ill that calls special attention to the politics of ideas and gives it a special poignancy. It is unlikely that a good politics can be pursued unless it is first imagined, and the legitimate role of identities, interests, and other influences are based in such conceptions. The worst political excesses are most fully recognized by such imagination, but more importantly, bad ideas can produce a bad politics, ranging from truly evil imagining to thoughts that are merely inaccurate, illogical, or incomplete.

Ideas can take many forms in politics. We can usefully describe this variation with a series of electrical metaphors, and the proverbial links between heat and light.

Sometimes the politics of ideas is like lightning, where the friction within public or private life generates a sudden and tumultuous disagreement. Such events fuel intense conflict, where opponents regard each other as worse than enemies and animosity feeds willful misunderstanding. Lightning literally sheds more heat than light, polarizing the participants and enhancing the prospects for violence. Such conflicts

1

are sometimes necessary, of course. If nothing else, good ideas must be defended, and a good politics can arise out of such a defense. But usually political lightning is counter-productive, wearing down the body politic with sound and fury, and in the end signifying nothing.

Sometimes the politics of ideas is like a dynamo, a regular and efficient generator of fuel for politics. Dynamos produce more light than heat, and their output can be harnessed for a variety of useful purposes. Here disagreement encourages debate on pressing questions and provides incentives for compromise and cooperation. In such extended conversations, opponents come to respect and understand one another, finding in their most serious differences a common calling and a higher purpose. Under these circumstances, ideas discipline and animate political identities, interests, and other influences, giving them meaning beyond themselves. Even when such dynamos fall far short of the ideal, they make public life more understandable and good government more likely.

At other times the politics of ideas is like a battery, where the fuel for politics flows from the past, stored up during previous periods of debate and discussion. Indeed, when a good politics infuses identities, interests, and other influences with meaning, it leaves behind the potential to secure its future. However, a politics powered only from the past eventually grows weak and ineffective, providing neither heat nor light. Lacking new energy with which to innovate, it becomes irrelevant to contemporary problems and increasingly unproductive. Opponents are committed to old arguments and well-rehearsed excuses, understanding one another all too well and having no goals beyond their habitual motions. Ultimately, dead batteries enervate the political process—so much so that citizens may yearn for lightning.

The essays in this book concern the importance of ideas—and the ideas of importance—to American politics at the beginning of a new century and a new millennium. On the one hand, the authors find a distressing absence of ideas in politics and a parallel rise in the power of political identities, interests, and other influences to the detriment of the body politic. And on the other hand, many of the ideas that are present are problematic, resembling intermittent lightning or drained batteries. All the authors argue, implicitly or explicitly, for new political dynamos to fuel a good politics in the next century.

A second and more controversial topic lies at the heart of the book: political parties should and can house such political dynamos. Some authors vigorously defend this proposition, while others dispute it on normative grounds and others are skeptical it can occur in the short run. This debate can be summarized under the rubric of four searches: for a public philosophy, party responsibility, party policy, and democratic citizenship.

The 2000 elections make these searches especially pressing. The Republicans and Democrats fought themselves to a virtual tie at every level, in what might be called the "one percent solution." The Republican presidential nominee, Texas Governor George W. Bush, won the Electoral College by less than one percent of the electoral vote (4 out of 538 votes), while his Democratic rival, Vice President Al Gore won the popular vote also by less than one percent (some 500,000 out of over 100 million votes cast). The Republicans retained control of the House of Representatives by just about the same margin (5 out of 435 seats), and the Democrats achieved a 50-50 tie in the Senate—with the GOP retaining some semblance of control by virtue of the potential tie-breaking vote of the Vice President. Similar tiny margins were recorded in state and local elections. Even the court system shared in the sharp division, with the dispute over presidential ballots in Florida resolved by a controversial 5-4 vote of the U.S. Supreme Court—following an equally controversial 4-3 vote in the Florida state Supreme Court.

The 2000 campaign was characterized by political lightening, especially in the post-election court battles in Florida. Certainly, the resolution of the dispute via the judiciary—for the first time in American history—produced more heat than light. In some respects, the campaign was one of the most partisan ever, with Bush and Gore taking on the stereotypes of their respective parties. Although a moderate on racial matters, Bush became an anathema to African-Americans, who voted nine-to-one for Gore. Likewise, devout Southern Baptist Gore was rejected by his fellow evangelical Protestants, and thus the entire South—including his home state of Tennessee—voted for Bush. Ironically, these and many other sharp divisions in the electorate occurred despite the fact that neither Bush nor Gore excited much popular enthusiasm, even among their own partisans. Despite the intensity of the campaign and record breaking expenditures, voter turnout edged up just above 50 percent of the eligible electorate. It seems as if the party's batteries were finally completely drained. Indeed, the 2000 election found the major political parties very far from dynamos in the politics of ideas. One possible bright spot was the relatively high issue content in the campaign, ranging from detailed budget blue prints to novel proposals to reform Social Security. Whether the closely divided government will allow any of these proposals to be seriously pursued remains to be seen.

THE SEARCH FOR A PUBLIC PHILOSOPHY

In the first essay, Wilson Carey McWilliams lays out the intellectual challenges confronting American politics at century's end. His essay begins with a contemporary paradox: the United States enjoys great prosperity and unrivaled power combined with a deep discontent with public life. The political standoff of the 2000 election underlines this paradox. This situation arises in part from the momentous economic and social changes within the country and around the world. As a consequence, the institutions of civil society have been fragmented, political organizations frayed, and governments discredited to an extraordinary degree. This decay of public life has tarnished the achievements of the age, from international preeminence to technological wizardry. And worse yet, it has made the task of coping with common concerns especially difficult, limiting the quality of American democracy. A special problem is the long-term effects of such a politics on the character of the American citizenry.

The fundamental problem, argues McWilliams, is not so much the lack of common values, but the lack of common dreams. Shorn of "grand public purposes," politics has become dominated by private philosophies, many of which have characterized the country since its founding. Identity politics and moral controversies such as abortion flash across the political landscape like political lightning. Meanwhile, the ponderous weight of private interests, buttressed by political-influence-as-usual, drains the last energy from political batteries charged in the distant past. In this context, the search for a public philosophy is critical because it is a first step in restoring a political dynamo to the politics of ideas.

Political parties are not a central focus of McWilliams' argument, but they appear at every turn. They are both casualties and culprits in the decay of public life. As with the government, economic and social change has undermined the social support for the major parties. Such trends debilitated party organizations and eventually undermined public allegiance to them. Part of the retreat from public life has been decreasing involvement and interest in elections by the citizenry. An array of institutional hurdles, such as the campaign finance laws, have hampered the ability of parties to respond to the challenges posed by these changes. However, the major parties have also contributed to these—and their own—problems. McWilliams agrees with the assessment that the major parties are "brain dead," as often captives of private philosophies as exponents of public ones. An implicit message in such criticism is that parties can play an important role in reinvigorating public life.

THE SEARCH FOR PARTY RESPONSIBILITY

The next two essays make McWilliams' implication explicit, debating the role that the major parties *should* play in the politics of ideas. In chapter 3, John White offers a cogent statement of a proposition widely held by scholars: stronger political parties are essential to a good politics. He then discusses the ways that parties might be strengthened, including changing public laws, political practices, and the ideas associated with them. White argues that stronger and more influential party organizations will improve the political process, especially if they pursue new ideas. Indeed, ideas are the crucial ingredient: citizens have lost interest in the major parties in large measure because they have failed to articulate clear ideas about the purposes of government. White shares much of McWilliams' criticism of the major parties: they often serve as conductors for lightning storms and otherwise run on an ancient and feeble current. But drawing on the concept of party responsibility, he fervently believes that the major parties should and can become political dynamos. To White, the 2000 election was a major disappointment.

In chapter 4, Everett Ladd offers a dissent from the scholarly consensus on parties, disagreeing with White on many points. Rejecting the
concept of party responsibility, he argues that the case for stronger,
responsible parties is based on the unarticulated assumption that a larger
government and expanded politics are desirable things. If these pre-
mises are not accepted—and Ladd argues that the electorate has em-
phatically rejected both in the 1990s—then the case for stronger parties
is seriously undermined. Ladd believes stronger and more programmatic parties are unlikely to resolve the discontent with public life
because party organizations and their ideological activists were an important cause of the discontent. He notes that the national party committees gained great organizational resources and programmatic content
precisely when the present decay of public life began.

In our terms, Ladd is skeptical of parties becoming political dynamos in the politics of ideas. Drawing on Tocqueville's notion of
"great" and "small" parties, he sees strong, principled parties as conductors of political lightning, convulsing society with "maximalist
politics," generating excessive heat and little light. In contrast, "small"
parties, characterized by weak organization and a lack of principle,
merely agitate society as they run down their political batteries. Ladd
is content with the current "mixed" party system, where ideas arise
from many sources within and outside of the parties, and the parties
themselves are not dynamos. Indeed, Ladd might have found considerable virtue in the 2000 election.

Thus, White and Ladd have a serious disagreement over the role
of parties, a dispute that should spark lively debate among party
scholars and political practitioners alike. But these differences should
not obscure an important point of agreement: both see ideas as a
critical element of a good politics. For White, greater party strength
and programmatic content will help reinvigorate public life, while
Ladd sees such factors as undermining it.

THE SEARCH FOR PARTY POLICY

Even if one agrees that parties should be political dynamos in the
politics of ideas, there is the question as to whether the major parties
can fulfill this task in the near future. A first step in this direction

would be the adoption of consistent policy positions by the Republicans and Democrats. The next two chapters review the intellectual debate within the major parties, identifying competing alternatives for party policy as the century draws to a close.

In chapter 5, John Pitney reviews the situation in the GOP. Using a religious and temporal metaphor, he finds three factions among Republicans, the "fundamentalist," "orthodox," and "reform." "Fundamentalist" Republicans believe the party has strayed from true conservatism and they want to return it to policies of the past. This faction includes the religious right, exemplified by Gary Bauer, but also economic nationalists, such as Pat Buchanan. "Orthodox" Republicans are conservative in the Burkean sense, favoring stability and caution over philosophy and vision. This faction is moderately conservative on most issues, seeking modest adjustments to the status quo. Representing the party "establishment" in name as well as temperament, this faction supplied Republican presidential nominees in the 1990s, President George H. Bush and Bob Dole. The "reform" Republicans are anxious to move forward, redefining future government and politics. This faction is reminiscent of the original Progressives of the early 20th century. Stressing market forces, individual choice, and decentralization, "reform" Republicans are a diverse lot, including in one way or another John McCain, Newt Gingrich, Jack Kemp, and Steve Forbes. Ironically, one of the biggest fans of "reform" Republicanism has been a Democrat, Bill Clinton.

Philip Klinkner reviews the intellectual foment among Democrats in chapter 6. His focus is on the "New Democrat" faction made famous by Bill Clinton and Al Gore. In many respects, this point of view has dominated debate in Democratic circles, proclaiming a "third way" between traditional liberalism and conservatism. Klinkner argues that there is much less to the "New Democrats" than meets the eye. While useful in the short run, this ideology has only a limited capacity to transform national politics in the future. He notes that the key themes of the New Democrats, responsibility, opportunity and decentralization, are remarkably similar to "modern" Republicans, such as Dwight Eisenhower (or Pitney's "reform" Republicans). Eventually, the Democrats will have to forge a more effective ideology, taking into account the various kinds of "old Democrats" and "progressives" still active in the party.

Can the major parties adopt coherent policies, given this welter of factions? Pitney and Klinkner imply that it may be possible. The "reform" Republicans may enjoy a breakthrough in the 2000 campaign with George W. Bush and "compassionate conservatism." Meanwhile, although the nomination struggle between Al Gore and Bill Bradley failed to transform the "New Democrat" ideology, Gore's narrow defeat may do so. Thus, both the "reform" Republicans and "New Democrats" may represent the foundations of future political dynamos in the politics of ideas. There are, however, reasons to believe such developments may not occur. Both parties have factions that can easily generate political lightning, such as the "fundamentalist" Republicans and their ideological opposites among the Democrats. And each party's establishment is characterized by factions running on old political batteries, including the "orthodox Republicans" and the various kinds of "old Democrats." If Klinkner is right, the "New Democrats" may simply be a version of "orthodox" Democrats; "reform" Republicans may suffer this fate as well.

THE SEARCH FOR DEMOCRATIC CITIZENSHIP

Of course, the success of any party policy depends on how well it resonates with the voters. This fact begs an important question: is the American citizenry capable of responding to the kind of policy positions that allow parties to be political dynamos in the politics of ideas? Put another way, does the citizenry have the appropriate "democratic" character? McWilliams raises this question in chapter 2, and Steve Schneck explores it in more detail in chapter 7.

Schneck points out that a successful democracy requires "remarkable" citizens with special skills and values. Such citizens are rare and must be cultivated. Democratic citizenship requires, at a minimum, the "mortgaging of private interests for the commonweal," and this trade does not come naturally to most Americans. Drawing on the debate between the Federalists and Anti-Federalists at the origins of the American party system, Schneck argues that American political parties have not been particularly effective at cultivating remarkable citizens. This situation arose in part because the Federalists won the initial contest and were able to influence the future pattern of party politics. In Schneck's view, the Federalists substituted "remarkable" citizens for a "remarkable" political process that replaced the need for virtue with a careful balance of political identities, interests, and other influences. The costs of this strategy are apparent in present-day politics of ideas: minorities of citizens are inflamed by political lightning and majorities are connected to dying political batteries. Indeed, the 2000 election was an example of both these problems.

Like the other authors, Schneck sees the major parties as victims of the excesses of private interest and an absence of public goals. And as the clash between the Federalists and Anti-Federalists reveals, the parties themselves have often been complicit in these problems. Their most serious failing is inadequate cultivation of "remarkable" citizens. After all, parties are uniquely situated to provide citizens with opportunities to develop democratic character by participating in meaningful dialogue and debate over pressing public questions. A good politics of ideas is central to such opportunity. When the major parties house political dynamos, they do more than power democracy, they empower future generations of democratic citizens.

When the history of the late twentieth century is written, one of the catch phrases of the period will surely be "ideas have consequences." But not all of the consequences of ideas are desirable or equally so. The politics of ideas can be political lightning, batteries, or dynamos. One of the most important debates facing the country is whether the major political parties can house political dynamos, or if we must search elsewhere for the fuel to power a good politics. The results of the 2000 election make this debate especially pressing.

NOTE

Earlier versions of chapters 2, 3, and 7 in this collection appeared in John Kenneth White and John C. Green (eds.) *The Politics of Ideas: Intellectual Challenges to the Major Parties After 1992* (Lanham, MD: Rowman & Littlefield, 1995).

2

The Search for
a Public Philosophy

WILSON CAREY MCWILLIAMS

Ending the millennium, the American republic is prosperous and unrivaled, its material power matching the New Rome of the Founders' imagining, but its public life marked by "discontents," or even a "lost soul."[1] The century's last year began with the president impeached before the bar of the Senate, but behind the headlines, it is American democracy that stands "on trial."[2]

Americans seem increasingly apt to regard government with suspicion, begrudging its authority. Policy makers, fearing to offend, walk on tiptoes. By contrast, party conflicts have grown bitter, but Theodore Lowi is right to call the parties "brain dead," lacking any public vision capable of calling for broad civic commitment or sacrifice.[3] And generally, in our political practice, we attach more and more limitations and qualifications to democratic institutions' moral title to rule.

Neither side in the abortion debate, for example, is willing to entrust the issue to majorities; the contenders volley salvos of competing "rights talk," each asserting that its position should be constitutionally protected against democratic politics.[4] "Identity politics"—which includes the demands of religious groups as well as those claiming to represent women, gays and lesbians, and racial or ethnic minorities—is not so much a claim to be *part* of the public as to be *separate* within it. Similarly, the major initiatives in education, following the example of a number of areas of public policy, appear to focus on lending public support to private or quasi-private institutions. Public authority, in part being "devolved" to states and localities, in a much more fundamental sense is being *dismantled.*[5]

11

The heart of American public philosophy has always been the quest for self-government.[6] Today, however, many Americans wonder whether self-government is really possible, or more precisely, whether it is worth the price. A considerable majority of us worry, too, that the American public is a "phantom," just as Walter Lippmann said more than seventy years ago.[7] Many see a fraying of the moral fabric of American life; to others, contemporary conflicts only reveal differences long suppressed or slighted. In fact, Americans have a remarkably common morality, but one defined in terms of essentially *private* decencies; their major public principle is a tolerance that reflects their despair of any public standards by which values and virtues may be evaluated.[8] In that sense, Americans have common values: what they are losing, as Todd Gitlin writes, is common dreams.[9] In our politics, public philosophy is increasingly reduced to whispers; the strong voice belongs to private philosophy expressed in and through public institutions. Yet this is also a familiar problem: the scales of our politics, delicately poised, have always tended to tip in a private direction, chronically needing—as they do today—statecraft and citizenship to right the balance.

For the American founders, public philosophy began with the teaching that human beings are naturally free, separate individuals who construct government to better fulfill their private purposes, primarily their desires for safety and well-being: the "first object" of government, Madison wrote, lies in protecting individual liberty and diversity. In this view, government exists to overcome the threats and obstacles posed by nature and by other humans; its positive aim is mastery, and hence the acquisition of power. But clearly, government so conceived can be dangerous to its creators, and the Framers' political science aims to check and channel government's dynamic in ways that make the "power house" compatible with individual variety and liberty.[10]

The goal of the public philosophy underlying the Constitution, then, is the effort to maximize both individual liberty and aggregate power. Government is measured by its utility in advancing our private interests, but also by two crucial public standards: (1) the goal of securing the rights of its citizens and (2) the principle that just authority derives from the "consent of the governed," a doctrine that at least points in the direction of democratic politics.

So conceived, government also was understood to rely on certain virtues beyond the calculations of interest. In the first place, the Framers recognized a need for honor, at least to the extent of keeping one's word, even when doing so no longer seems in one's interest, because "promises, covenants and oaths," in their theorizing, are the fundamental "bonds of human society."[11] The success of political society, they reasoned, makes citizens ever more prone to forget the harsh necessity that drove human beings under governance. We are all tempted to believe that we are clever enough to evade some laws without being detected, or that others will not imitate our lawlessness, or at least that the potential gains outweigh the risks. That danger is especially great among the poor, the obscure, and the oppressed—or private persons generally—who may easily feel that what they do will go unnoticed, or that they have little to lose. (President Clinton's lapses, of course, show that even the most public people are also vulnerable to such notions.) With reason, the "obligation of contracts" has special status as the only duty mentioned in the Constitution, saving the oaths of high officials, and the founding generation hoped that Americans would see promise-keeping as a sacred duty.[12]

Second, the American founders relied on the readiness of citizens to defend their rights even at the price of comfort or safety, including their willingness to risk or sacrifice their lives to preserve the rightful freedom of others. They never doubted, in other words, that republican citizenship calls for at least some ability to subordinate the body and its goods to what the soul loves and regards as worthy.[13]

Third, the founding generation expected and desired citizens to be influenced by generosity of spirit, especially in caring for the helpless and dependent. Locke took it as a vital argument for revealed religion that reason and interest had not persuaded even the most civilized ancients that it is criminal to kill one's children by exposing them.[14] Most of the Framers would have agreed, and all of them would have insisted on a morality that recognizes the claims of humanity.[15]

Finally, they looked to economic life to provide the material bases of civic morality and freedom. In Jefferson's well-known thesis, abundant land peopled by small proprietors meant a public capable of avoiding the economic dependence that can easily lead to political servility.[16] More important, Jefferson later observed that, given labor scarcity, even those who worked for wages could expect a "satisfactory situation," so that they enjoyed a citizen's portion of independence. In this argument, income is not the critical factor, although a socially adequate wage is clearly a part of what Jefferson had in mind: by itself, relative affluence can make workers even more dependent on their employers. Political independence turns, rather, on the security of employment, the worker's confidence that adequate employment will be available, so that no particular employer is essential to his or her livelihood.[17] Economic inequality, under these conditions, is roughly compatible with political equality, but that coexistence is always uneasy and a matter for public concern.

The Framers' design, consequently, relied on civil society—on families, churches, communities, and economic life—to provide the moral and psychological basis of republican citizenship. Preoccupation with "mere life," Aristotle argued, is essentially a private philosophy, not genuinely free because driven by the body and its desires. Public life grows naturally out of the human yearning for a "good life" beyond material satisfactions, and especially out of the desire for a voice in shaping the conditions and directions of life, self-government's freedom beyond price.[18] The Framers trusted that civil society would provide the crucial intermediate step, the ability to think and feel beyond the limits of self-interest that is the precondition of public spirit and public philosophy alike.

But although they relied on civil society to provide the characterological foundations of citizenship, the Framers gave it no explicit recognition. The Constitution speaks only of states and individuals; it is silent about civil institutions, taking them more or less for granted. If anything, the Framers were concerned about *limiting* the authority of states and localities in the service of individual freedom. The highest laws, and hence the highest forms of public speech, acknowledge individual liberty as a public principle, but not the claims of families, churches, and communities.[19] The long-term problem of this imbalance seemed clear to Tocqueville: allied with the authority of the laws, the "spirit of liberty" would play an increasingly strong role in shaping the "habits of the heart." Americans,

Tocqueville wrote, tended to justify their actions in terms of "self-interest rightly understood" as the all-but-universal language of public morality. Tocqueville acknowledged the advantages of this way of speaking, but he also noted that it was misleading: in fact, Americans often acted from motives that were more generous and public spirited, but seemed embarrassed to admit it: "they are more anxious to do honor to their philosophy than to themselves." That American public philosophy—the doctrine that all human beings act from interest—was preempting public speech meant that the ideal of self-sacrifice and civic spirit would become increasingly voiceless, locked in the private silences of the soul.[20]

Today, Tocqueville's prophecies are mirrored in American public life. Culturally and morally, we are considerably more diverse than we were in the past, and what once could be taken for granted now inspires dissent. At the same time, it is important to remember that America was *always* diverse, and a good deal more various than appearances suggested, since the expression of that diversity was constrained by public opinion and authority. Now, as we have observed, the majority of Americans incline to regard morality, even when beliefs are widely shared, as an essentially private matter. They are apt to say that morality is "relative," and that we should not "judge" or "impose" on the sincerely held convictions of others. At least in public speech, a gentle individualism is sweeping the field.[21] Reflecting a broad unwillingness to hurt others, this persuasion also shows little inclination to *help* them. Conceived in these terms, the public plays a weak hand in any contest with private interest, falling short of even the limited standard of civic spirit the Framers set for republican government.

More than words is involved: all our institutions, civil and political, are being unsettled, their power reduced, their authority questioned.[22] New technologies and new forms of economic life—most obviously, "globalization" and the "information revolution"—are shaking or shattering relationships and the order of communities and nationalities. Old forms and organizations seem increasingly outdated and irrelevant.[23] Yet while the past grows more distant from our experience, the future becomes unimaginable: Americans find it prudent to go cautiously, limiting—if not avoiding—their commitments to place, relationships, or moralities.[24]

But while these developments privatize us psychologically, they also make us more interdependent. Private life, John Dewey argued, is defined by matters that are our "own business," having few if any consequences beyond the individuals immediately concerned; public affairs include acts that have important consequences for relatively distant others.[25] In these terms, as more and more of our lives become integrated by economics and technology, the less there is that can be called purely private or local: my business is too deeply affected by yours, and by the great, seemingly impersonal processes of communication and the market.[26] These intrusions of the public sphere, however, emphasize our weakness and vulnerability, and make us more eager for the consolation of those private spaces that remain. Tocqueville saw the principle clearly enough: an expanding public pushes us, psychologically, in the direction of an ever more isolated individualism.[27]

It only accentuates matters, of course, that "domestic insecurity"—the term is Theodore Lowi's—is the ordering principle of so much of social and economic life.[28] Jefferson's confidence in a democratizing economy does not match our experience. For a quarter century, real wages for hourly workers have tended to fall, and working families have kept up only by having more family members work, by taking extra jobs, or by working longer hours.[29] Worse, work itself has become increasingly unreliable: "downsizing" layoffs and the increase in part-time and temporary employment have created an anxious workplace notable for a decline in loyalty between employees and employers, and among employees themselves—possibly "leaner," Kristin Downey Grimsley writes, but "definitely meaner."[30] A rising concern for money and for private interest, as W. Lance Bennett observes, is "a realistic response to an unpredictable economy defined by job and career instability."[31] As Jefferson would have warned, the price of insecure employment and inadequate wages is a decline in "social capital" and public spirit that even threatens basic civility.[32] The comparative well-being of the last few years only heightens worries about the future: the electorate's unwillingness to rock the boat, so evident in recent campaigns, testifies less to a complacent moderation than to a desperate sense that things could easily be worse.

In recent elections, in fact, America's growing economic inequality has been a suppressed issue, treated like an improper story in polite company. (In the presidential primaries of 2000, Senator John McCain at least acknowledged the problem, if inadequately; the Democratic contestants, Vice President Gore and former Senator Bradley spoke of the need to help the poor, but only skirted the broader issue.) Yet the disparity among Americans, already the greatest among industrial countries, is becoming still greater, threatening to create a two-tier market and a two-tier society.[33] Even people like Mickey Kaus, who regards fairly extreme inequality of income as inevitable and acceptable, recognize that it undermines the sense of being one people with a common destiny.[34]

Like the economy, upper-income Americans are increasingly international, with weaker ties to place and to particular communities. The "underclass," by contrast, is minutely local, trapped in relatively confined neighborhoods by a lack of jobs, skills, and resources. And between those poles, the middle sectors have been losing ground.[35] Middle-class Americans prefer, understandably enough, to see their fortunes as linked to those of the well-to-do, a disposition that helped fuel the right-leaning politics of the '80s, with its emphasis on opportunity. That tendency has been reinforced by the recent escalation of the stock market, which touches—disproportionately—so many Americans. But this feeling of prosperity, present or prospective, is evidently uneasy. In movie theaters and on Broadway, Americans in the millions have been engrossed by the story of the *Titanic*, seeing in that old disaster, I think, a cautionary tale for our time: the great ship was characterized by radical inequality; in its aborted voyage, humanity was sacrificed to the goals of speed and profit; its technological wonders were entrusted to very imperfect humans. And it is also suggestive that the *Titanic*, shadowed by nemesis, sank in 1912, in the heyday of the Progressive era.

In fact, in the embattlement of the contemporary middle class, E. J. Dionne sees the basis for a new progressivism.[36] There are stirrings that support his view, more a matter of motion than an organized movement, but capable of great power: consider the assault on smoking and the tobacco industry so reminiscent of the temperance movement a century ago, or the political weight of environmentalism and the concern for historic preservation, which parallel the old Progressive zeal for conservation. On both the right and the left, moreover, legions of Americans seek to invoke government's support for what they take to be a just order of domesticity and social life, a goal which was the *leitmotif* of the Progressive movement.[37] In a stumbling, half-articulate way, great numbers of Americans are looking to politics to shore up or reconstruct the foundations of civil life.

Across the political spectrum, however, Americans have very little trust in government. Many citizens see government—massive and impersonal—as only another of the overwhelming powers that are shaping their lives, dimly comprehended and presumptively malign. More Americans, probably, regard government as proverbially bumbling and inefficient, and millions hold both views in an uneasy synthesis.

Even those who think of government more positively are bound to suspect that it matters less, that it possesses only a shrinking ability to rule. Capital and jobs, technology and information—and with them, plagues and terrorists—cross and recross national borders in ways that seem increasingly beyond government's control. In the nineteenth century, international capital—through institutions like banks and the gold standard—called the tune in much of national economic policy-making, but today the effects of globalization are more pervasive, reaching even into once-inviolate areas of life.[38] In this much at least, Marx and Engels look to have been right: the dynamics of capitalism have "drawn from under the feet of industry the national ground on which it stood."[39]

In critical areas, government itself appears to agree: American antitrust policy, for example, has grown more tolerant of megamergers, based on the argument that competition must be seen in terms of the international market, in which such combinations are necessary to permit American corporations to hold their own against giant foreign and quasi-foreign rivals. Even if accurate, however, this analysis is limited to the *economic* effects of consolidation: it ignores the consequences of concentrated economic power for democratic politics, probably because policymakers are assuming that politics must adapt itself to the logic of the market. It is no wonder, then, that so many Americans, as Bennett notes, see government as "at worst, responsible for the economic conditions that dominate their private lives and, at best, of little use for remedying them."[40]

Loyalty to large-scale institutions, however, depends decisively on their ability to act effectively. Nations and mass parties are inevitably somewhat impersonal, complex collectivities in which public policy depends on compromise: their moral claims have always lacked luster when compared to those of more intimate and more coherent communities. It is not surprising, then, that identification with nations and parties has been declining in Europe and the United States.[41]

Challenges to elites and authorities—refusals to "work within the system"—have become a feature of contemporary politics, more routine than remarkable.[42] That style fits a society in which rapid technological transformations unsettle *old* elites, but immediately create *new* ones, endowed with power—for the moment, until the next round of change—but without institutional or moral ties to most citizens.[43]

Political allegiances, consequently, show signs of fragmenting. Political fashion features "identity politics," which—by emphasizing different experiences and unique perspectives—points first to groups (most insistently, genders, races, and sexual orientations), but ultimately to individuals. Organized group membership, accordingly, is declining in favor of "networks" and volunteering, styles of participation—fluid, informal, often intense, but relatively episodic—in which civic involvement is shaped to the mood and convenience of individuals.[44] And, as Gilles Lipovetsky saw in the French student movement of 1968, this sort of individualized, designer politics, even in its radical versions, is essentially reactive in its rhythms: outbursts of activity in response to events succeeded by periods of withdrawal. It lacks the sense of obligation, the persistent devotion to an idea of the public good, that is at least possible in unions, parties, and formal political organizations generally.[45] Once again, Lance Bennett is on the mark: a great deal of what currently passes for political activity is largely driven by "socially dislocated individuals seeking social recognition and credible representation for their personal concerns," a defensible goal but one that falls short of genuinely public life.[46]

We continue, however, to have a vital stake in public policies, and the more we depend on or care about particular public programs, the less willing we are to let majorities decide their fate. The importance of *government* becomes an argument against democratic *politics*, public policy argues against public life. Citizens are less inclined to rely on electoral politics, which demands the aggregation of money and mass support.[47] Instead, they seek to have their favored policies defined as "rights" protected by courts and administrative agencies, tribunals where it is possible to wage one's *own* politics with comparatively little help from others. In this kind of politics, lawyers and accountants are probably needed as champions, but these are people we *hire*, and their fees, however high, are not apt to come close to the cost of an electoral campaign.[48] It is also a remedial and negative politics, aimed at protecting one's interests and damaging one's enemies; as the Paula Jones case shows, litigation can do that even without winning—to the extent, in that instance, of unsettling the verdict of an election. And in general, to the degree that political issues are decided elsewhere, democratic politics is reduced—at best—to entertainment, something between a sitcom and a soap opera.

Certainly, that describes politics in 1998, dominated as it was by the president's "inappropriate relationship" with Monica Lewinsky. Majority opinion, which consistently supported President Clinton, was relatively sensible, but its very immunity to the scandal emphasizes the privatization of public life.[49] Most Americans find the president's conduct reprehensible; they do not trust him or respect him as a person. Nevertheless, they are persuaded that he is doing a "good job" because the country is prosperous and at peace, making few demands on our considerable comforts. They see the president as like an attorney, a technician engaged to further our private ends, someone whose skill matters but whose moral character is largely irrelevant. (In fact, too much rectitude might put the president at a disadvantage in any contest with rogues.) Great *public* goals, however, call on citizens to change habits and make sacrifices, running risks and enduring discomforts that presume trust, not only in the craft of leaders, but in their moral direction. That Bill Clinton is not evaluated in those terms indicates how little we expect from public life.

There is, however, another side to American opinion. Baffled and battered by colossal forces, most of us yearn for some greater degree of human control over human artifacts, especially since it is once again becoming clear that the market, left to itself, goes to extremes, undermining its social roots and threatening an economic "meltdown."[50] Millions of us want, at least, someone to blame or hold responsible for the course of events, which helps account for the extraordinary range and popularity of conspiracy theories: notably, worries about a "New World Order" and its supposed covert masters.[51] That impulse can easily slide into an eagerness for someone to "take charge," as in the movie *Independence Day*, a temptation that sits uncomfortably with constitutional rule. But at the bottom of all these responses is the very human desire to be treated with dignity and to have a say, the itch for self-government that—given the manifold weaknesses of individuals—can only be satisfied in politics.

Through most of the last two decades, political memories have been dominated by events that testify to the limits of politics—Vietnam and Watergate, the disappointments of the Great Society, and the collapse of Soviet communism—and opinion, here and abroad, has tended to disparage and turn away from government. Jimmy Carter was as much a part of that move toward privatization as Ronald Reagan, but its master spirit was Margaret Thatcher, with her iron willingness to let the market shatter society, embracing inequality in the confidence that economic dynamism would eventually build a new and better order.

In the '90s, however, the wind changed. Electorates turned more doubtful about the direction of things and tiptoed, with many fits and starts, toward government as a defender of families, civil society, and values "beyond the dreams of avarice."[52] In Europe, electorates leaned to the left, but in India, a similar—though more threatening—impulse brought the Hindu nationalists to power. In Benjamin Barber's terms, if the result was not always "jihad," there was no mistaking the uneasiness with "McWorld."[53]

In America, the mood has been even more uncertain and ambivalent, but the signs are clear: no fire, but plenty of political smoke. Social conservatism has been a portent, although a muddled one. Detesting '60s liberalism, social conservatives have allied themselves with the opponents of "big government," but they also despise media culture and are at least half-aware that the moral teaching of the market, on its own terms, is a self-seeking relativism. At least at the local and state level, conservatism champions an extended view of government's office as a defender of moral order, an attitude that conservatives often—even regularly—extend into national politics.[54] And on the other side of the spectrum, Bill Clinton's 1992 promise of a "New Covenant" appealed to fairly ambitious hopes—vaguely, to be sure, and in his usual soft tones—before the failures of his early presidency led him to settle for "third-way" politics, mild humanitarianism linked to enthusiasm for technology and international trade.[55] Still, the policy of substituting work for welfare—even in the harsh form passed by Congress and signed by the president—reflects the conviction that government should support the moral discipline and civic dignity of labor. A gentler inclination toward the rehabilitation of government, moreover, is evident in the strengthening of the electorate's long-standing sympathy for public programs like education, health care, and the environment. That disposition—and the perception that the Republican Congress was obsessed to the point of inaction by the scandal surrounding the president—contributed to the surprising result of the 1998 election. And among public intellectuals, more and stronger voices are acknowledging the perennial human need for political community.[56]

So far, however, these developments are not much more than offstage murmurs; in the theater of American politics, the high drama is the danger to democratic life. Aristotle warned that in defining a regime, the *form* of rule may be deceptive: its real character lies in its implicit public philosophy, its evaluation of the *claims to and obligations of citizenship*. The heart of democracy, he held, is not "rule by the many"—although that is clearly an element of democratic governance—so much as the belief that the contribution to public life that matters is a freely given life. What deserves to rule, in democratic teaching, is love of country, the willingness, if need be, to sacrifice everything to preserve its self-government, a gift the poor can offer as well as any. Government by majority, by contrast, can also be *oligarchic* if political society presumes that the highest public good is material prosperity, so that wealth deserves a stronger voice, and special consideration, in public councils.[57]

All commercial societies have at least some tendency toward that oligarchic public philosophy; these days, in the United States, the tilt is all too visible. In the absence of serious campaign reform, public office is increasingly limited to the wealthy or those who can enlist their support. Money is not a sufficient claim to rule—Californians, for example, defeated both Michael Huffington and Al Cecchi—but it is virtually a necessary one, and fund-raising consumes more and more of the time and attention of public servants. And it is part of the same current that prosperity and well-being have so high a rank in American lives, and in our judgment of goods and presidents.

Democratic public philosophy points to the need to redress the political balance, strengthening the links between citizens and their government in order to make self-government seem less a matter of form and fable and more an everyday possibility. That agenda requires rebuilding confidence that democratic institutions are more than shams: a first item, obviously, is policy effectively reducing the power of money in elections (a goal that probably necessitates a Supreme Court willing to reverse its insistence, in *Buckley v. Valeo*, on the free speech rights of wealth against the government's right to protect relatively equal access to public forums).[58] It also calls for expanding the opportunities for effective participation, encouraging local party organizations, political associations, and the skills and habits of democratic deliberation.[59]

Beyond laws and structures, however, democratic citizenship and politics rely heavily on democratic souls, on the moral qualities Tocqueville described as "habits of the heart."[60] In the contemporary quest for a public philosophy, this is a matter of controversy: many pluralists—and democratic theorists of other schools—argue that it is unnecessary and undesirable, as well as impossible, for Americans to expect common first principles or foundations. Such "non-foundational" thinkers argue that we should accept the fact of diversity and different perspectives as a starting point, looking for public principles and policies to *emerge* from democratic debate and discussion, as the endpoints of a political process, subject to continuing challenge and reformulation rather than limiting preconditions.[61]

Yet theorists of this persuasion characteristically presume that politics will be inclusive, making room for all voices, and that speech will be civil, respecting (and possibly, celebrating) the differences of others. Inclusive civility, however, is hardly a given in human affairs, and "nonfoundationalist" doctrines, on their own terms, provide no basis for regarding it as normative, beyond the very uncertain calculations of utility. In fact, "nonfoundational" ideas of deliberation *rely* on certain foundations and fundamentals, norms of inclusion and respect that derive from religious precepts like the Golden Rule (or at least, their Kantian equivalents). Similarly, democratic institutions rest on a hard teaching: the egalitarian convention by which the minority, however wise or strong, agrees to be governed by the majority's vote. These convictions and conventions can never be taken for granted, and certainly not in our time.[62]

Samuel Bowles and Herbert Gintis point to a humanly natural basis for public philosophy, a disposition to cooperate and to be generous with one's fellows, a "strong reciprocity" that leads individuals to make sacrifices and to act against self-interest, narrowly defined, in the service of community. Bowles and Gintis emphasize that this is not altruism: human beings expect their fellows to make appropriate contributions to the common good. Recognizing that self-interest is *always* a temptation, and that it is sure to be the ruling principle of at least a minority, most people are acutely aware of the risk that "free riders"—both those who take too much and those who give too little, the "welfare cheat" and the tax-evading elite—will undermine public spirit. Liberals, at least in recent years, have underrated the extent to which an insistence on punishing free riders—on seeing contribution as a *duty*—is a vital element of civic generosity.[63]

But conservatives have their own purblindness. On the right, public intellectuals have been prone to argue that, if government would get out of the way, civil society would be revitalized and would be able to remoralize society in general. But the institutions of civil society, battered by social change, need to be helped, not left on their own. As Bowles and Gintis point out, greater social distance among people—and hence, any increase in the scale, diversity, or inequality of political society—makes it difficult for them to assert or protect common values, since they are dealing with others they don't know, and who cannot be controlled effectively by informal sanctions and rewards. In large and diverse societies, consequently, civil society cannot defend its own commonalities: it needs the formal sanctions and authority of government.[64]

In its pursuit of justice, public philosophy necessarily involves a debate—the centerpiece of democratic contestation—about which contributions are most deserving. Its premise, however, is the duty and right of every citizen to make an appropriate contribution to the common life, a goal that includes the attempt to make good the shortcomings of the economy and society. It is the task of public philosophy, consequently, to assure and demand—for and from all of us in contemporary America—dignified work, a fair share of taxes, and the opportunity to serve. (Transforming Bill Clinton's rather anemic Americorps into a universal program of national service might be a place to begin.)[65]

Human beings are not born free, but indebted; their identities are more defined by what they owe than by what they own.[66] In that sense, the possibilities of human liberty—and the first principles of public philosophy—turn on our right to reduce that debt.

NOTES

1. Michael Sandel, *Democracy's Discontents: America in Search of a Public Philosophy* (Cambridge: Harvard University Press, 1996); John P. Diggins, *The Lost Soul of American Politics* (Chicago: University of Chicago Press, 1986). The imagery of a New Rome among the American founders is described in James S. Young, *The Washington Community, 1800–1828* (New York: Columbia University Press, 1986).

2. Jean Bethke Elshtain, *Democracy on Trial* (New York: Basic Books, 1995).

3. Theodore J. Lowi, "Toward a Responsible Three-Party System," chap. 3 in Theodore J. Lowi and Joseph Romance, *A Republic of Parties: Debating the Two-Party System* (Lanham: Rowman and Littlefield, 1998), 3.

4. Mary Ann Glendon, *Rights Talk: The Impoverishment of Political Discourse* (New York: Basic Books, 1991).

5. Theodore J. Lowi, "Think Globally, Lose Locally," *Boston Review*, April/May 1998, 4–10.

6. Michael Sandel, "America's Search for a New Public Philosophy," *Atlantic Monthly*, March 1996, 58.

7. Walter Lippmann, *The Phantom Public* (New York: Macmillan, 1925).

8. Alan Wolfe, *One Nation After All* (New York: Viking, 1998).

9. Todd Gitlin, *The Twilight of Common Dreams* (New York: Henry Holt, 1995).

10. Madison's comments are made in *The Federalist* #10. The reference to the "power house" is taken from Henry Adams, *The Education of Henry Adams* (Boston: Houghton Mifflin, 1961), 421.

11. John Locke, *A Letter Concerning Toleration* (Indianapolis: Bobbs Merrill, 1955), 52.

12. Article 1, section 10; on the general point, see Wilson C. McWilliams, "In Good Faith: On the Foundations of American Politics," *Humanities in Society* 6 (1983): 32–35.

13. As Harvey Mansfield writes, "it can easily be in one's interest to accept satisfaction at the cost of one's freedom" whenever that freedom is "costly or irksome or dangerous." *America's Constitutional Soul* (Baltimore: Johns Hopkins University Press, 1991), 82.

14. John Locke, *The Reasonableness of Christianity*, ed. I.T. Ramsey (Stanford: Stanford University Press, 1958), 64.

15. Many of the founders, of course, believed in a "moral sense" or instinct, more or less inherent in the body. See Jefferson's Letter to Peter Carr, August 10, 1787, and his Letter to Thomas Law, June 13, 1814, in *Life and Selected Writings of Thomas Jefferson*, ed. Adrienne Koch and William Peden (New York: Modern Library, 1944), 430–431, 638–639.

16. *Notes on Virginia* and Letter to John Jay, August 23, 1785, *Life and Selected Writings of Thomas Jefferson*, 280, 377.

17. Letter to John Adams, October 28, 1813, *Life and Selected Writings of Thomas Jefferson*, 633.

18. Aristotle, *Politics*, 1252b8-1253a3.

19. Strikingly, the Preamble to the Constitution refers to "posterity," but not to *family*.

20. Alexis de Tocqueville, *Democracy in America* (New York: Knopf, 1980), II:121–125.

21. Wolfe, *One Nation After All*; Robert Bellah et al., *Habits of the Heart* (Berkeley and Los Angeles: University of California Press), 1985.

22. Hannah Arendt, *Crises of the Republic* (New York: Harcourt Brace, 1969), 69.

23. Ithiel deSola Pool, *Technologies without Boundaries* (Cambridge: Harvard University Press, 1990); fixed forms and relations are visibly undermined, Marx and Engels wrote: "All that is solid melts into air." *The Communist Manifesto* (London: Penguin, 1985), 83.

24. Robert Putnam, "Bowling Alone: America's Declining Social Capital," *Journal of Democracy* 6 (1995): 65–78; Tocqueville, *Democracy in America*, II:98-99.

25. John Dewey, *The Public and its Problems* (New York: Holt, 1927).

26. Consider the Court's argument in *Wickard v.Filburn* 317 US 111 (1942).

27. Tocqueville, *Democracy in America*, II:215-216.

28. Lowi, "Think Globally, Lose Locally," 10.

29. Barry Bluestone and Stephen Rose, "Overworked and Underemployed," *American Prospect*, March/April 1997, 59, 60, 67.

30. Kristin Downey Grimsley, "Leaner and Definitely Meaner," *Washington Post National Weekly*, July 20–27, 1998, 21; W. Lance Bennett, "The

Uncivil Culture: Communication, Identity and the Rise of Lifestyle Politics," *PS* 31 (1998): 750–753.

31. Bennett, 751.

32. Putnam, 669; Bluestone and Rose, 69.

33. Jeff Gates, "The Ownership Solution," *Boston Review*, December 1998/January 1999, 32–33.

34. Mickey Kaus, *The End of Equality* (New York: Basic Books, 1992).

35. Gates, 33.

36. E.J. Dionne, Jr., *They Only Look Dead: Why Progressives Will Dominate the Next Political Era.* (New York: Simon and Schuster, 1996).

37. Robert Wiebe, *The Search for Order, 1877–1920* (New York: Hill and Wang, 1966).

38. Karl Polanyi, *The Great Transformation* (Boston: Beacon, 1957).

39. *The Communist Manifesto*, 83.

40. Bennett, 758.

41. Ronald Inglehart, *Modernization and Postmodernization* (Princeton: Princeton University Press, 1997), 304–305, 311.

42. Inglehart, 295–296, 298–305, 307–323.

43. Jacques Ellul, *The Technological Society* (New York: Vintage, 1964), 208–218; James Lardner recently pointed out that radio, too, was acclaimed as a "flattener of hierarchy" that would provide "unprecedented access to information" and end isolation. "Ask Radio Historians About the Internet," *U.S. News and World Report*, January 25, 1999, 48.

44. Bennett, 745, 747.

45. Gilles Lipovetsky, "May '68, or the Rise of Transpolitical Individualism," trans. L. Maguire, in *New French Thought*, ed. Mark Lilla (Princeton: Princeton University Press, 1994), 214, 218.

46. Bennett, 755.

47. Benjamin Ginsberg and Martin Shefter, *Politics By Other Means* (New York: Basic Books, 1990).

48. Marc K. Landy and Martin A. Levin, eds., *The New Politics of Public Policy* (Baltimore: Johns Hopkins University Press, 1995).

49. John Zaller, "Monica Lewinsky's Contribution to Political Science," *PS* 31 (1998): 182–189.

50. The phrase is Theodore Lowi's. "Think Globally, Lose Locally," 8.

51. Pat Robertson, *The New World Order* (Dallas: Word, 1991). This helps explain the peculiar excess of right-wing reactions to Bill Clinton, raising that weak man to demonic stature.

52. The phrase is taken from Russell Kirk, *Beyond the Dreams of Avarice* (Chicago: Regnery, 1956).

53. Benjamin R. Barber, *Jihad vs. McWorld: How Globalism and Tribalism Are Reshaping the World* (New York: Ballantine, 1996). On European developments, see Roger Cohen, "A Matter of Trust for Europe," *New York Times*, January 31, 1999, WK1 (one of a pair of articles under the headline, "Voters All Over Take the Wheel from Conservatives.)"

54. Lowi, "Think Globally, Lose Locally." Conservative recognition of the moral defects of the market is especially marked among the students of Leo Strauss.

55. Stephen Skowronek, "The Risks of 'Third-Way' Politics," *Society*, September/October, 1996, 32–36. On American developments generally, see Richard L. Berke, "An Identity Crisis in the U.S.," *New York Times*, January 31, 1999, WK1 (the second of the paired articles mentioned in note 53, supra).

56. Rogers Smith, *Civic Ideals* (New Haven: Yale University Press, 1997); Amitai Etzioni, *The New Golden Rule: Community and Morality in Democratic Society* (New York: Basic Books, 1996).

57. Aristotle, *Politics*, 1279a11–1281a11.

58. *Buckley v. Valeo*, 424 US 1 (1976); Scott Turow, "The Supreme Court's Twenty-Year-Old Mistake," *New York Times*, October 12, 1997, WK15.

59. For example, Amy Gutmann and Dennis Thompson, *Democracy and Disagreement* (Cambridge: Harvard University Press, 1996).

60. Tocqueville, *Democracy in America*, I:299.

61. Iris Marion Young, *Justice and the Politics of Difference* (Princeton: Princeton University Press, 1990), 227–228, 238–240.

62. Young, 191, 236; Smith, *Civic Ideals*, 486; Nancy Rosenblum, *Membership and Morals: the Personal Uses of Pluralism in America* (Princeton: Princeton University Press, 1998), 35.

63. Samuel Bowles and Herbert Gintis, "Is Equality Passé?" *Boston Review*, December 1998/January 1999, 4–7; Stanley C. Brubaker, "Can Liberals Punish?" *American Political Science Review* 82 (1988): 821–836.

64. Bowles and Gintis, 7–8.

65. For example, see Edmund Phelps, *Reworking Work* (Cambridge: Harvard University Press, 1997).

66. Bertrand de Jouvenel, *Sovereignty*, trans. J.F. Huntington (Indianapolis: Liberty Fund, 1997), 316–317.

3

Reviving the Political Parties: What Must Be Done?

JOHN KENNETH WHITE

In the film *Primary Colors*, the youthful character based on the real-life Clinton staffer George Stephanopoulos makes an impassioned argument to the wife of Governor Jack Stanton (the stand-ins for Hillary and Bill Clinton) for wanting to back a presidential candidate who upholds lofty ideals:

> I was always curious about how it would be to work with someone who actually cared. . . . It couldn't always have been the way it is now. It must have been very different when my grandfather was alive. Hey, you were there. You had Kennedy. I didn't. I've never heard a president use words like "destiny" and "sacrifice" without thinking bullshit. OK, maybe it was bullshit with Kennedy, too. But people believed it. And I guess that's what I want. I want to believe it. I want to be a part of something that's part of history.[1]

The search for "true believers" is not confined to those on the Left. In a dramatic presentation before the U.S. Senate advocating the real-life impeachment of President Clinton, House Judiciary Chairman Henry Hyde defended the righteousness of his conservative cause: "Equal justice under the law is what moves me and animates me and consumes me. And I'm willing to lose my seat any day in the week rather than sell out on those issues. Despite all the polls and the hostile editorials, America is hungry for people who believe in something. You may disagree with us, but we believe in something."[2]

Following the Cold War, shouts from both ends of the ideological spectrum for Americans to start believing in something have become increasingly louder and more commonplace. In September 1998, Bill and Hillary Clinton asked Democrats to adopt a "Third Way" of thinking about politics. Both believed that the Third Way could command broad public support because the government they envisioned would be fiscally prudent, even as it empowered ordinary citizens. Addressing an audience of world leaders that included British Prime Minister Tony Blair and Italian Prime Minister Romano Prodi, the Clintons maintained that public service could be inspiring, even as liberalism abandoned large-scale bureaucracies in favor of creative public/private partnerships. Anthony Giddens, director of the London School of Economics, complemented the Clintons for their insight: "The Third Way agenda, to which Bill and Hillary Clinton have made a fundamental contribution, is the new agenda for our time. Third Way politics will dominate the next twenty to thirty years in the way that welfare reformism dominated after World War II and neoliberalism has dominated over the past twenty to thirty years. We are talking about a very fundamental paradigm shift."[3]

But the First Couple's plea for a Third Way that could inspire a John F. Kennedy-like season of public service, was overshadowed on the very day of their speech-making by the grainy televised picture of Bill Clinton testifying about his adulterous affair with White House intern Monica Lewinsky. For months, the Clinton-Lewinsky scandal dominated the headlines and was *the* topic of discussion on most cable news programs. Mrs. Clinton, who wanted to become known for her ability to inspire women to enter the political realm, won plaudits instead for standing by her man. Perhaps Hillary Clinton's most famous appearance as First Lady was on NBC's *Today* show when she told host Matt Lauer that "a vast right-wing conspiracy" was to blame for l'affaire Lewinsky.[4] By leading the charge against her husband's enemies, Mrs. Clinton recast herself from a hard-nosed advocate of women's liberation into a wronged woman who became the most admired figure to emerge from the Clinton-Lewinsky scandal. One-third of the public came to hold a more favorable view of the First Lady, and most attributed their change of heart to the stalwart defense she gave her husband.[5] By the spring of 1999, the public dialogue had shifted away from scandal to speculation (encouraged by the First Lady) that she would seek a U.S. Senate seat from New York.

Mrs. Clinton may be the only "winner" to emerge from the long impeachment saga that has sullied the Clinton presidency. Surely, those Democrats and Republicans who manned the front lines of the impeachment war were certain losers. Shortly after the Senate trial ended, just 23 percent of those polled said the Republican party was addressing important problems, while 35 percent thought that was true of the Democrats.[6] A widespread perception took hold that both parties had lost touch with the voters. In a CBS News/*New York Times* survey taken days before the 1998 balloting, fewer than half chose either major party as best able to keep the nation prosperous, uphold family values, or reduce crime. Likewise, majorities withheld support when asked which party "cares about people like yourself," "has higher ethical standards," is "more likely to reduce taxes," or "has the better ideas for leading the nation into the 21st century."[7] Instead of heeding the voters' demand to "get on with it" and dismiss the impeachment articles in favor of a censure, Clinton, the Republican-controlled Congress, and Independent Counsel Kenneth Starr became locked in a death struggle that alienated an already disdainful electorate. As one New York schoolteacher put it: "I don't think the [Starr] investigation is going to end anytime soon. They'll find something else to draw it out a little longer. I've lost all faith in the process. It's like a circus."[8]

The disconnect between Washington elites who thought Clinton should be ousted and the desire for continuity and stability in the hinterlands only increased the hatred many Americans felt toward politics and politicians. Just after the 1998 balloting, 54 percent agreed with the proposition that two-party politics reflects "the isolated agenda of the establishment."[9] Repeatedly, the public has registered its discontent with politics-as-usual by giving unusually high support to unconventional office-seekers. Five times in the past three decades, third party presidential candidates have shared a portion of the limelight with the major party contenders: George Wallace (1968), John Anderson (1980), Ross Perot (1992 and 1996), and Ralph Nader and Pat Buchanan (2000). Nader, it can be said, cost Democrat Al Gore the White House.

At the state level, third parties have been especially active. Inspired by Ross Perot, the Minnesota Reform Party scored a major upset in 1998 by winning that state's governorship. Minnesotans rejected Democrat Hubert H. Humphrey III (son of the late vice president) and Republican candidate Norm Coleman (the mayor of St. Paul) in favor of former pro wrestler and radio talk show host Jesse ("The Body") Ventura. Much of Ventura's appeal lay in his colorful persona, which many saw as a necessary corrective to a corrupt, scandal-based politics. When asked how he would fare as governor—especially since the state legislature has one house controlled by the Democrats and another held by the Republicans—Ventura, who now uses the moniker "The Mind," responded: "Well, I think it's an advantage because now you're truly getting a three-prong approach, aren't you? You're getting the head executive to be neutral from the other two parties, and the two parties—one controls the House, one controls the Senate, and I will act as a mediator to bring them together and do what's best for Minnesota and cut out the partisan politicking. And like I said in my campaign, let's put Minnesotans first. There's more of us than there are Democrats and Republicans. And, obviously, I was right, wasn't I?"[10] Ventura had a point: 36 percent said Ventura's upset victory provided additional "evidence of a serious trend in the country away from major parties."[11]

As Ventura intimated, Americans have often eschewed traditional two-party politics because they see character as the only qualification needed to hold public office. According to one 1986 poll, 92 percent agreed with the statement "I always vote for the person I think best, regardless of what party they belong to."[12] The Founding Fathers were the first to espouse the view that "character counts." They rejected partisanship as an inevitable debasement of the civic culture (a view echoed by substantial majorities during the impeachment saga). In his 1796 Farewell Address, George Washington warned that parties "tend to render Alien to each other those who ought to be bound together by fraternal affection." He accused parties of hindering government by making it "the Mirror of the ill-concerted in incongruous objects of faction, rather than the organ of consistent and wholesome plans digested by common councils and modified by mutual interests."[13] In Washington's view, character, not party loyalty, should determine who is fit for public office. Only a few years earlier, in the *Federalist Papers*, Treasury Secretary Alexander Hamilton agreed with Washington and declared that if "characters pre-eminent for ability and virtue" won the presidency, that would be enough to permit them to act in the public interest.[14] Ironically, while Washington was dispensing his warning against partisan politics, Hamilton was busily forming his own political party to advance his economic and foreign policies.

Still, Washington's warning has persisted through the centuries. Each year, the partisan members of Congress (all 535 of whom except two belong to a major political party) assemble to hear Washington's famous words read to them once more. Character has become embedded in the mythology of the presidency. Parson Weems started it all with his *The Life and Memorable Actions of George Washington.* The 1806 edition of the book contains the apocryphal tale of Washington chopping down the cherry tree and refusing to lie about it. To this day, children still read about that mythical cherry tree. Likewise, their parents have a similar need to hear their presidents tell them once more about those heroes who remain devoted to country, family, and community. Ever since the Reagan era, State of the Union Addresses have been used to tell these tales of heroism, as presidents recognize their heroes sitting above them in the House gallery.[15] One reaction to the Clinton-Lewinsky scandal is a heightened appeal for those who espouse traditional family values. According to one survey, 71 percent *agree strongly* with the statement: "This country would have many fewer problems if there were more emphasis on traditional family values."[16] John McCain's success in the 2000 New Hampshire primary punctuated public longing for new heroes.

But the Clinton scandals and the intense media scrutiny to which all presidents in the Information Age have been subjected means that the presidency is no longer a place where heroes are likely to be found. Americans realize this: 66 percent of those who left the polls on Electon Day 2000 said they do *not* want their child to grow up to be president.[17] Inspirational leadership may come from sports, the popular culture, or in the serialized stories of ordinary citizens doing extraordinary things. But heroic tales are scarce in today's politics.

Rather than heroes, it is the political Svengalis who are extolled for their brilliant tactics. Republican Ralph Reed became celebrated as the brilliant strategist who ran the Christian Coalition. Even better known was the Clinton team of George Stephanopoulos, James Carville, and Dick Morris. The case of pollster Morris is especially interesting, since he received substantial credit for Clinton's 1996 win, despite having once worked for conservative Republican Senators Trent Lott and Jesse Helms. In 1997, House Minority Leader Richard Gephardt took aim at Clinton's attentiveness to Machiavelli-like characters such as Morris, telling his fellow Democrats that they must become a party "where principles trump tactics."[18] But Gephardt's warning was drowned out in the intense partisan shouting match that surrounded Clinton's impeachment. Even Gephardt became caught up in the rhetoric, deriding the "politics of personal destruction."[19]

Gephardt's description of 1990s politics as "the politics of personal destruction" points to a phenomenon that has become readily evident in the impeachment-tarred Clinton era. Scandal-based politics has become a new form of entertainment in which Democrats and Republicans pursue their mutually destructive jihads. In the early days of the Clinton-Lewinsky scandal, Democratic strategist James Carville appeared on *Meet the Press* and declared "war" on independent counsel Kenneth Starr.[20] Carville's wife, Republican Mary Matalin, was strongly pro-impeachment and the couple enjoyed appearing on the Sunday talk shows to air their differences. Their notoriety stemmed as much from the entertainment value of a married couple holding opposite political views and their willingness to air them as from their political skills.

The media is only one player in the new era of scandal-based politics. Suzanne Garment of the conservative American Enterprise Institute writes that scandal politics is controlled by a "self-enforcing scandal machine" that includes the parties, courts, and news media as active political players: "Prosecutors use journalists to publicize criminal cases [involving members of the administration] while journalists through their news stories, put pressure on prosecutors for still more action."[21] Scandal politics has transformed our once firmly based party politics into a new form of media entertainment. Programs such as *Entertainment Tonight, Inside Edition,* and *Inside Hollywood* covered the Clinton-Lewinsky scandal with as much verve as the more conventional news outlets.

In this media-dominated climate of scandal and battle, the case *for* political parties has become more unpopular than ever. Throughout much of American history, voters have disliked parties—even as political scientists and some politicians have extolled them. Our eighth president, Martin Van Buren, believed that parties were noble instruments of public service: "It has always . . . struck me as more honorable and manly and more in harmony with the character of our people and of our institutions to deal with the subject of political parties in a sincerer and wiser spirit—to recognize their necessity, to prove and to elevate the principles and objects to our own [party] and to support it faithfully."[22] Near the end of the nineteenth century, historian James Bryce devoted 200 laudatory pages to parties in his masterpiece, *The American Commonwealth*: "Parties are inevitable. No large country has been without them. No-one has shown how representative government could be worked without them. They bring order out of chaos to a multitude of voters."[23]

In the twentieth century, the case for parties made by the new discipline of political science became even more vehement. In 1950, the Committee on Political Parties, a distinguished group having the imprimatur of the American Political Science Association, issued a report entitled *Toward a More Responsible Two-Party System*. In it, the committee set forth a premise that became dogma: "Throughout this report political parties are treated as indispensable instruments of government."[24] In the decades that followed, political scientists accepted the inevitability of parties and assigned several desirable characteristics to them. Giovanni Sartori claimed they were "*the* central intermediate structures between society and government."[25] In 1977, Everett Carll Ladd used strong language to defend his pro-party position: "Modern government is an incredibly complex instrument. It has so many different parts responsive to so many different interests that the natural centrifugal pressures are well-nigh irresistible. Party is the one acceptable counteracting centripetal force—and not only at the national level, but in the states and cities as well.[26] The Committee for Party Renewal (CPR), a bipartisan organization consisting of academics and party activists, declared in 1976: "Without parties there can be no organized and coherent politics. When politics lacks coherence, there can be no accountable democracy. The stakes are no less than that."[27]

As executive director of the Committee for Party Renewal, I made the case in 1991 for political parties before a hostile Sam Gejdenson, then chairman of the House Task Force on Campaign Finance Reform. The views I espoused, which reflected the conventional wisdom of my colleagues, were immediately challenged by the Connecticut Democratic congressman:

WHITE: I think there is a larger purpose involved generically with political parties, period, which is they mobilize people to action. No one does it . . . no other single interest group does that the way the parties do.

GEJDENSON: Maybe they should. I don't know if they do. But why should they do it with taxpayer dollars?

WHITE: Let me just say—You know, you mentioned what your obligation was to political parties. Let me just offer that the Democratic Party in Connecticut tendered you their nomination, as did the Democratic.

GEJDENSON: No, no. That's not how it happened. They tendered the nomination to somebody else. I went out and got the people's support, and then I . . . won the nomination in a primary. . . . But why should the taxpayers, or why should the government, give [the parties] free television time to strengthen or weaken their hold? Why should it be their business?[28]

Just as the lack of a party connection between those "inside the Beltway" and those outside it has made politics irrelevant, so, too, is there a disconnect between scholars who view parties as necessary instruments of governance and voters whose decisions are described by late twentieth century party scholars as "anomalies" (since the electorate seems to take some delight in consistently rejecting their pet theories—especially party realignment[29]). Put bluntly, political scientists view parties as essential for a vibrant democracy, but voters do not. Because parties no longer command much attention at the ballot box, divided government—the inevitable result of individual decisions made about particular candidates—has become the norm. During the nineteenth century, divided government was a rarity—once having happened when Andrew Johnson assumed the presidency following Lincoln's assassination (Lincoln had placed Johnson on his "Union Party" ticket in 1864), and again when Grover Cleveland lost public confidence in 1894. In each case, the "anomaly" was quickly corrected by a subsequent election producing unified party rule. However, since 1954, divided government of nearly every permutation has been tried. Throughout the Cold War, it was the Republicans who captured the presidency (thanks to their patriotic appeals and abhorrence of communism) while Democrats retained their New Deal congressional majorities.[30] After a brief fling with unified party government during the first two years of the Clinton administration, voters gave the GOP a congressional majority for the first time in forty years, even as they later opted to keep Clinton in office (a decision they consistently reaffirmed during the long impeachment struggle). Divided government is so commonplace that it reaches into nearly every nook and cranny of the continental United States. In 2000, for example, voters in Vermont, Rhode Island, and Pennsylvania backed Democrat Al Gore, while at the same time choosing Republican U.S. Senate candidates by large margins. While the 2000 contested results produced the first unified party government since 1993, the Republican position was especially precarious, and most pundits expect the GOP to lose its congressional majorities in 2002.

Despite considerable voter antipathy toward parties, and the inability of party leaders to inspire much confidence, an academic debate still rages over how to revitalize party-based politics. Many agree with Herbert Agar, who defended political parties as forming "the heart of the unwritten constitution [that] help the written one to work."[31] Ralph M. Goldman, president of the Center for Party Development, authored an article whose title summarizes the lamentations of pro-party activists: "Who Speaks for the Political Parties or, Martin Van Buren, Where Are You When We Need You?"[32] From these pro-party perspectives have come three strategies designed to advance the cause of party renewal: (1) change the laws, (2) change the players, and (3) change ideas.

CHANGE THE LAWS

Political scientist Leon D. Epstein likens parties to public utilities since both are embedded in the laws and are duly regulated by government.[33] State laws define political parties, impose requirements for ballot access, and prescribe their organization. Because parties are so deeply embedded in the statutes, any danger that the Democrats or

Republicans will expire, as the Whig Party did during the 1850s, is extremely remote.

The fact that national and state governments claim parental rights to the parties gives legislatures and the courts ample opportunities to give them succor. By expanding the powers of parties in the law, and enhancing their "rights" in the courts, a strategy has been advanced whereby party renewal can take place. The Supreme Court has emerged as a pivotal institution in this fight. In *Tashjian v. Republican Party of Connecticut* (1986), the Court articulated a "right of association" that gives parties considerable latitude in designing their bylaws—even if those provisions run contrary to existing state law. The case arose when Connecticut Republicans, adopted a rule allowing registered independents to vote in primaries for federal and state offices. (Connecticut law permitted only registered Republicans to participate in GOP primaries.) The Court sided with the state Republicans, saying they had a "right of association"—even if this right was used to de-value party membership. The latter point was made in a withering dissent by Justice Antonin Scalia:

> The Connecticut voter who, while steadfastly refusing to reg-
> ister as a Republican, casts a vote in the Republican primary,
> forms no more meaningful an "association" with the Party
> than does the independent or the registered Democrat who
> responds to questions by a Republican Party pollster. If the
> concept of freedom of association is extended to such casual
> contacts, it ceases to be of any analytic use.[34]

Nonetheless, the "right of association" was reaffirmed and enhanced in *March Fong Eu v. San Francisco County Democratic Central Committee* (1990). This Supreme Court case centered on the oppressive laws governing California's many political parties—most of them adopted in the 1970s by the state legislature. These statutes determined the terms and qualifications for party officers, forced parties to organize on countywide bases, prohibited them from endorsing candidates, and even mandated that party chairs alternate between northern and southern California. (When Jerry Brown became state Democratic chair in the mid-1980s, he rented an apartment in San Francisco so as to comply with the existing law.) Speaking for a unanimous Court, Justice Thurgood Marshall declared: "Freedom of association means not only that an individual voter has the right to associate with the political party of her choice, but also that a political party has a right to identify the people who constitute the association, and to select a standard-bearer who best represents the party's ideologies and preferences."[35] With that statement, parties were emancipated from oppressive state regulations and, if they wished, could write their own bylaws (as Massachusetts Democrats did in 1979) that would strengthen party organizations.

The Supreme Court reaffirmed its pro-party stance in 1996. In *Colorado Republican Federal Campaign Committee and Douglas Jones, Treasurer v. Federal Election Commission*, the Court allowed political parties to raise and spend unlimited sums of so-called "soft money" to attack the positions advocated by the opposing party and its officeholders. The case stemmed from a 1986 Colorado U.S. Senate contest in which Timothy Wirth, the Democratic incumbent, charged the state Republicans with violating federal law by airing radio commercials criticizing his stance on the issues. The Court concluded that because the Republican party did not have a Senate candidate at the time the advertisements were purchased (April 1986), any prohibition on party-sponsored radio advertisements constituted a violation of the First Amendment's right to free speech. Speaking for a majority on the Court, Justice Stephen Breyer wrote: "The independent expression of a political party's views is 'core' First Amendment activity no less than is the independent expression of individuals, candidates, or other political committees."[36]

In the *Eu* and *Colorado* cases, the Committee for Party Renewal (my loyalties to which I have already alluded) played an important role. The California CPR chapter raised the money and provided the wherewithal to pursue the *Eu* case before the state and federal courts, ending with a favorable decision at the U.S. Supreme Court. In the *Colorado* case, the executive board of the committee filed an amicus curiae brief before the Supreme Court defending the right of parties to raise and collect money on behalf of their candidates and issue positions. The committee argued that such money instead of corrupting was some of the cleanest money in politics since it was used for issue advocacy. The Federal Election Commission had argued that restraints on money were necessary to staunch the flow of corrupt dollars into the political system. Justice Clarence Thomas cited the committee's brief favorably in agreeing with the thrust of the Court's decision.[37]

Having been instrumental in helping devise the Committee for Party Renewal's strategy for using the courts as a means for furthering the party's cause, I must also acknowledge the dangers inherent in such an approach. In 1990, the same Supreme Court that sided with the parties in *Tashjian, Eu,* and *Colorado Republicans* voted to strip the parties of their last vestige of power: patronage. In *Rutan v. Republican Party of Illinois,* Justice William Brennan articulated the Court's preference for nonpartisanship: "To the victor belong only those spoils that may be constitutionally obtained. . . . A government's interest in securing effective employees can be met by discharging, demoting, or transferring staff members whose work is deficient."[38] In a biting dissent Justice Scalia wrote that by taking aim at political parties, the Court inadvertently had targeted itself: "If there is any category of jobs for whose performance party affiliation is not an appropriate requirement, it is the job of being a judge, where partisanship is not only unneeded but positively undesirable. It is, however, rare that a federal administration of one party will appoint a judge from another party. And it has always been rare. Thus, the new principle that the Court today announces will be enforced by a corps of judges (the Members of this Court included) who overwhelmingly owe their office to its violation. Something must be wrong here, and I suggest it is the Court."[39]

Relying on the courts to revive parties is ironic because the pro-party arguments hinge on a "politics of rights." Of course, parties have associational rights guaranteed by the First and Fourteenth Amendments. But by asserting these "rights," party advocates necessarily neglect the voters, who, after all, were the reason parties were supposedly formed in the first place. It is the parties that organize ballots *for* voters, clarify issues *for* voters, and perform important civic functions *for* voters. By engaging in a "politics of rights," parties assert a nonnegotiable absolute that leaves little room for compromise. Moreover, in these cases the party advocates are the justices of the Supreme Court—arguably the least democratic institution of our government.

CHANGE THE PLAYERS

Another strategy for reform is to give parties a seat at the election game. By making the parties players again, prospective presidential nominees presumably would have to pay attention to them. One way to accomplish this is to rewrite federal and state laws governing the parties, as well as state party bylaws. This can be done by (1) altering the presidential nominating process to allow for pre-primary conventions; (2) fashioning (or refashioning) state party charters to permit a greater role for activists; and (3) reforming campaign finance laws to give parties a greater role in collecting and disseminating scarce campaign dollars.

After the disastrous 1968 Democratic Convention, both parties fell victim to the so-called McGovern-Fraser reforms. Concerned about the Chicago riots and worried that the Democratic party was excluding too many women, young people, and blacks, the McGovern-Fraser Commission undertook the vital task of reform. In effect, the commission told the party establishment to "reform or else." The nomination process needed to be more *open, timely, and representative* of the wishes of average Democrats. As McGovern recalled: "In public statements, speeches and interviews, I drove home the contention that the Democratic party had but two choices: reform or death."[40] The McGovern-Fraser Commission arrived at a similar conclusion, telling Democrats it was past time to change their ways: "If we are not an open party; if we do not represent the demands of change, then the danger is not that the people will go to the Republican party; it is that there will no longer be a way for people committed to orderly change to fulfill their needs and desires within our traditional political system. It is that they will turn to third and fourth party politics or the anti-politics of the street."[41]

But by taking the job of determining a presidential nominee away from the "party regulars" and giving it to fickle primary electorates, Democrats suffered. Ever since 1968, their presidential candidates (save Walter Mondale and Al Gore) have had few, if any, ties to the party establishment. Jimmy Carter once derided the Democratic National Committee as "an albatross around my neck." Bill Clinton adopted the strategy of "triangulation" devised by his consultant Dick Morris in which he separated himself from congressional Democrats and Republicans. Because the party establishment is often excluded in making the presidential choice, one suggestion is to have a national primary preceded by party conventions designed to narrow the field of candidates.

A presidential pre-primary convention is not a novel idea.[42] It is used to make gubernatorial and other nominations in several states— including Connecticut, Massachusetts, and New York. Under this system, national conventions would convene in January of the election year. Anyone failing to receive 15 percent (some suggest 20 percent) of the delegate ballots would not qualify for a national primary to be held in June. Delegates to the one-day convention would include members of Congress, governors, state party chairs, and other party designees. The convention would act as a gatekeeper, screening out minor and fringe candidates who lack significant intraparty support. Such a system requires candidates to seek backing from all party members: first, among officeholders; later, from the rank-and-file who make the final determination of the party nominee.[43]

Another idea is to change the Electoral College, a cry that was heard once more after the 2000 presidential contest when the winner of the popular vote might not have become president.[44] Junking the Electoral College is a popular notion, but among its "unforeseen" consequences would be removing parties once and for all from presidential campaigns. I believe the Electoral College should be changed, but only modestly so by adding an addendum already in effect in Maine and Nebraska: allow a state to apportion its electoral votes, with one going to the winner of each congressional district and the two remaining "at large" votes going to the candidate receiving the most popular votes statewide. Such a system would not only meet the public test of "fairness," but would nationalize campaigns and encourage presidential nominees to campaign alongside congressional candidates.

To call presidential campaigns national contests is to employ a misnomer. In Campaign 2000, Vice President Al Gore ignored most "safe" Democratic states, including Massachusetts, Rhode Island, Connecticut, and even California. Instead, Gore and his Republican rival George W. Bush battled for votes in the nation's industrial heartland.

Permitting presidential candidates to win electors from congressional districts would encourage more national campaigning. Some recent examples make the case. In 1988, the Dukakis campaign left Florida at the end of September. Under my "October scenario," Dukakis would have won electors from Miami and some surrounding areas, and would have been encouraged to continue campaigning in the Sunshine State—especially in "swing" congressional districts. But realizing that Florida was lost, Dukakis was forced under the present system to seek precious electoral votes elsewhere. Similarly, in 1992 and 1996, Republican nominees George Bush and Bob Dole abandoned California by mid-October—ceding the state's precious fifty-four electors to Bill Clinton. Had California permitted its electors to divide their ballots by congressional district, Bush and Dole would have continued to campaign there. Had this proportional electoral vote system been in effect in 2000, Al Gore would have spent more time in Texas trying to cherry pick a few electors, instead of visiting the state only to raise cash from Democratic donors and then leave to take his fight elsewhere. Likewise, George W. Bush would have campaigned more aggressively in New York State alongside Republican Rick Lazio in an attempt to win some electoral votes there.

The change I propose can be accomplished without amending the U.S. Constitution—a simple alteration of state law would do.[45] By targeting congressional districts and media markets, candidates would be encouraged to campaign alongside their congressional counterparts. This is quite different from the deliberate distancing from political parties that modern presidential politicking encourages. Seeking reelection in 1972, Richard Nixon instructed his staff not to include the word "Republican" in any of his television advertisements or campaign brochures. Four years later Gerald Ford was advised not to campaign for Republican candidates lest his support erode among independents and ticket-splitters: "Any *support* given to a GOP candidate must be done in a manner to *avoid* national media attention."[46] In 1996, Bill Clinton devoted *one line* in his acceptance speech to making a case for unified Democratic party control of the federal government. By having congressional districts vote for president, the prospects for responsible party government would be enhanced.

Another suggested change is to have state parties write charters giving them a greater role in selecting candidates. Massachusetts Democrats did this in 1979, restoring the state convention to prominence.[47] Under its charter, prospective nominees must win 15 percent of the convention ballots to qualify for the primary. The charter also created local party caucuses that choose delegates to nominating conventions and "issues conventions" (the latter held in the off year). In the 1982 rematch between former governor Michael Dukakis and incumbent Edward King, the state Democratic party was an important player. Both candidates had to pay attention to the party machinery—and did so. Moreover, another candidate failed to receive 15 percent of the votes at the convention, and his inability to qualify for the primary probably determined the election outcome.[48]

Changing campaign finance laws to allow for a greater party role is also desirable. The Committee for Party Renewal has outlined six suggestions for reform:

1. Substantially increase existing limits on individual party contributions and thereby encourage party-building activities such as voter registration, program development, research, and get-out-the-vote drives.

2. Allow individuals to give more money to parties than to candidates.

3. Permit parties to make unlimited campaign contributions to candidates for all offices at all levels of government and channel such funds through existing party committees.

4. Provide full public disclosure of all party contributions and expenditures.

5. Mandate significant and free television time for parties to speak on behalf of themselves and their candidates. The television time would allow parties to promote their tickets and sponsor "generic" ads that convey positions on important issues and provide ample opportunities for individual candidates to be seen and heard. The content of such messages should be left completely to the parties and candidates.

6. Give parties sole sponsorship of all candidate debates. The free television time mentioned above should be contingent on the acceptance by the major parties of such sponsorship.[49]

In presenting the committee's views before the House Task Force on Campaign Finance Reform, I argued that these initiatives would restore parties to their "rightful place" in the political process, encourage two-party competition, stimulate public participation, and educate the electorate. I continue to believe that a campaign finance bill incorporating CPR's recommendations would accomplish these vital objectives.

But changing the presidential nominating system, altering the Electoral College, or changing campaign finance laws will *not* revive the parties. Indeed, changing either the laws or the players is inadequate to the task at hand because each of these strategies lacks a necessary ingredient for party renewal—the voters. In most debates about party renewal, political scientists and voters often talk past each other. Academics describe parties in reverential tones, extolling them for their civic virtues. We all know the story: after immigrants swarmed ashore, beginning in the 1840s with the Irish and the Germans, and followed in the 1890s by their southern and eastern European cousins, parties did a remarkable job in assimilating the newcomers into "the American way of life."

As noted at the beginning of this chapter, voters do not like parties, yet this was not always so. An apocryphal tale is told among Irish Americans of a Mrs. O'Reilly being driven to the polls one election day by her son James. Mrs. O'Reilly, who is seventy years old, has always sided with the Democrats. James, who is forty-five and has obtained some financial success, votes Democratic more often than not, but sometimes will vote Republican. James asks his mother how she plans to vote and is given the predictable reply: "Straight Democratic."

"Mom," says her frustrated son, "If Jesus Christ came back to earth and ran as a Republican, you'd vote against Him."

"Hush!" replies Mrs. O'Reilly. "Why should He change His party after all these years?"[50]

In the late nineteenth and early twentieth centuries, there were a lot of Mrs. O'Reillys. Back then, Americans tolerated parties—some even liked them. The right candidate and party can provide inspiration. This was powerfully demonstrated in the McKinley-Bryan contest. A check of railroad records shows that during the fall of 1896 approximately 750,000 people journeyed to Republican William McKinley's hometown of Canton, Ohio, to see the "front-porch" candidate. That figure represents *more than 12 percent* of McKinley's total vote. Likewise, when the Democrats nominated Al Smith for president in 1928, thousands of immigrants flocked to see their "first son." In Boston, 750,000 filled the streets—as many as saw McKinley during the *entire* 1896 campaign. The *Boston Evening Globe* reported: "No Boston crowd before ever went so mad. No other man ever called up such fervent joyous tumult of emotion from the deep wells of the heart of the city as this best-loved son of American city life."[51] Smith later wrote, "So intense was the feeling, so large the throng, that at times I feared for the safety of Mrs. Smith riding with me in the automobile."[52]

In those campaigns, voters liked parties for their ideas and believed that they were a means of empowerment. But that was then, and this is now. Today there are many more voters who sympathize with Mrs. O'Reilly's son James. Simply put, most voters do not like political parties. *And they are right not to like them.* They want compelling ideas and candidates whose stories resonate with their own experiences and aspirations. Parties are currently failing miserably in these tasks, and Ross Perot's garnering of 19 percent of the ballots in 1992 and 8 percent in 1996—enough to qualify the Reform Party for federal financing in 2000—speaks to the point. Only by reviving the parties from above *and* below will they be restored to their "rightful place."

CHANGE IDEAS

Back in 1986, Michael Horowitz, then an official in the Reagan Office of Management and Budget, worked in a spacious office in the Old Executive Office Building. Horowitz proudly showed a reporter around his luxurious digs, admiring the stunning view of the White House next door. At one point, Horowitz grabbed the reporter and said, "Look out that window. Do you know how I got here? Ideas. Ideas do count. Ideas move nations."[53]

Ideas, not laws, money, or rules, form the basis on which political parties exist. When I speak of "ideas," I mean such large concepts such as Franklin Roosevelt's belief that big government can help alleviate the plight of the dispossessed, or Ronald Reagan's adage that "government is not the solution to our problems; government is the problem." Without large energizing ideas, parties grow weak to the point of death. Some years ago, historian Henry Adams said of the Whigs: "Of all the parties that have existed in the United States, the famous Whig Party was the most feeble in ideas."[54] Parties cannot afford to be "idea-free" like some decaffeinated soft drink. But today Democrats and Republicans are engaged in a frantic search for ideas—realizing that something is missing in their relationship with the electorate. So far, both have little to show for their efforts.

The Republicans: After the Cold War, What?

The search for an energizing idea is a relatively new undertaking for Republicans. By the late 1990s, the GOP confronted the oldest conundrum in American politics: what to do after a major success? The Cold War provided the Republicans with an escape hatch from oblivion following the triumphs of the New Deal. From 1952 to 1988, the GOP won the presidency seven times in ten tries. "Peace through strength" became a shorthand for building a large defense apparatus at home that provided many with employment and projected American nationalism across the globe. The GOP's militant anticommunism, forged in the aftermath of the 1948 election defeat, the Korean War, and McCarthyism, brought the party's disparate elements together as never before. As long as the Russian bear prowled the woods (as was once depicted in a famous 1984 Reagan television advertisement), Richard Nixon, Ronald Reagan, Barry Goldwater, Pat Robertson, Pat Buchanan, George Bush, Bob Dole, and Dan Quayle could peacefully coexist.[55]

But when the Russian bear expired, Republicans experienced a profound letdown. In a book published shortly before his death in 1994, Richard Nixon forecast trouble ahead: "Historically, there is always a period of exhaustion after a military victory. Victory in the Cold War was not just military. It was a complex ideological, political, and economic triumph. Our exhaustion is therefore felt in all these dimensions simultaneously."[56] Absent a mission and a purpose, Republicans began to devour each other. In 1992, Pat Buchanan revived the Republican party's isolationist wing, which once had been represented by the "America First" movement and later by Ohio Senator Robert Taft. Buchanan embarrassed George Bush in the 1992 New Hampshire primary, winning 37 percent of the vote. Four years later, he decisively beat the establishment party candidate, Senate Majority Leader Bob Dole, in the Granite State. The disappearance of communism means that foreign policy has reverted back to what it was nearly a century ago—where arguments about tariffs and trade reverberate into the echo chamber of politics.

As if this were not enough, the Republican party finds itself engaged in a bitter struggle with the Christian Right. To be sure, the Christian Right's desire to return to the social conformity of the 1950s strikes a responsive chord with some. Working dads and stay-at-home moms perceive the GOP as the party that can best enhance traditional family values. According to a March 1999 *Washington Post/ ABC News* survey, 43 percent trusted the Republicans could do a better job of encouraging high moral standards and values; just 30 percent chose the Democrats.[57] Despite the pro-Republican "values gap," one problem lingers: traditional two-parent families no longer form a majority of the American electorate. In 1998 and again in 2000, Democrats *lost* among those who were white (both male and female); married; had incomes between $30,000 and $75,000; and had children under age eighteen. Using this rubric, Republicans won broad support from the mythical Ozzie and Harriet Nelson and Ward and June Cleavers. The 1998 defeat forced Newt Gingrich to resign the Speakership and his House seat. Two years later, George W. Bush's strong support among the mythical Nelsons and Cleavers helped make the election close. But changing demographics—i.e., fewer white, married couples with children under age eighteen at home—meant that the 2000 election would be won among the new faces that comprise a growing segment of the electorate: single mothers, Hispanics, Asians, and those who are divorced, or are gay, or whose definition of family is quite different from those families depicted in *The Adventures of Ozzie and Harriet* or *Leave It to Beaver.* This was especially true in Florida where a polyglot of minorities transformed what should have been an easy Bush win into a bitter court fight.

Adding to the Republican plight are serious intraparty divisions on economic issues. Ronald Reagan lent his powerful voice to the supply-siders, who maintained that tax cuts would result in an economic expansion that would reduce the federal budget deficits. Reagan implemented his tax and budget cuts with mixed results. The economy did grow, but at the expense of a $4 *trillion* federal deficit. Reagan maintained that these gargantuan deficits would force his Democratic successor to forego any attempt to resurrect Franklin Roosevelt's New Deal or Lyndon Johnson's Great Society. Bill Clinton's failure to enact health care reform in 1993 proved Reagan right. During the Reagan-Bush years, balance-the-budget conservatives, still rooted in their hatred of Roosevelt and Johnson, were appalled at the fiscal imbalances, but they kept quiet as long as the economy remained strong and the Soviet Union was a real threat. Senate Finance Committee Chairman Bob Dole, an old-fashioned fiscal conservative, often told the tale of a bus filled with supply-siders that had gone over a cliff. The tragedy, Dole quipped, was that there were three empty seats.

Balancing the federal budget, a feat that occurred during the second Clinton term, presented the Republican party with its biggest test since the end of the Cold War. Once more, success threatened the future of the GOP. Americans were pleased that the divided government they instituted in 1994 had produced the desired results. Clinton's economic plan was toughened by the Republican emphasis on budget-cutting. Now with the federal ledgers balanced, Clinton put all of his tactical skills to work—declaring in his 1997 State of the Union Address that any surplus must be used to finance Social Security and Medicare until he and the Republican-controlled Congress could agree on a plan to rescue these hallmarks of the New Deal and Great Society. Supply-siders argued that without a tax cut the GOP would be bereft of its biggest post-Cold War mission—reducing the size of government. A coterie of Republicans led by 1996 presidential candidate Steve Forbes and House Majority Leader Dick Armey wanted to junk the tax code altogether and replace it with a flat tax (a move that was greeted with considerable public skepticism and little Republican enthusiasm). Still other Republicans wanted to use the surplus to reduce the national debt. Another contingent preferred targeted tax cuts designed to help the Nelsons and the Cleavers. This group sensed that Clinton was winning the argument, and that the public no longer had the same resentments toward government that fueled the Reagan Revolution of the 1980s. Added to the mix were those congressional Republicans who, having had a taste of majority status, wanted to dispense some of the newfound federal largesse to their districts. The result was Republican inaction on the budget in

1998, and an omnibus bill that gave Clinton virtually all of the spending increases he wanted. Senator Charles Grassley, a balance-the-budget conservative from Iowa, recently declared: "I'm impressed with how difficult it is to manage the surplus. It's almost as difficult as managing the deficit."[58]

Adding to the GOP's woes is the dismal perception of the Republican party in the wake of its yearlong effort to impeach Bill Clinton. By March 1999, 56 percent disapproved of the job done by congressional Republicans; 40 percent approved. Democrats salivated at the prospect of winning control of the House in 2000, and voters seem inclined to reward them: 51 percent approve of how congressional Democrats have conducted themselves; 42 percent disapprove.[59] Republicans also suffered from the perception that their party was controlled by extremists: 39 percent said the Republicans were "too conservative," 41 percent thought its views were "about right," and just 15 percent said the party was "too liberal." Four years earlier, only 31 percent said the GOP's views were "too conservative," 54 percent said the party's views were "about right," and 11 percent thought they were "too liberal." Finally, by a 55 percent to 36 percent margin, Americans wanted the GOP to pick leaders that were more moderate in their temperament.[60]

The perception that the GOP is now the "impeachment party" has been aided by its association with Clinton's most vehement enemies. Independent Counsel Kenneth Starr is a reviled public figure: 60 percent thought he should cease and desist in his pursuit of Clinton and 58 percent thought he had gone too far in using his prosecutorial weapons.[61] As Clinton strategist James Carville said of Starr: "How could you have a better guy there? You've got a guy investigating you that two-thirds of the country hates. How could you be better?"[62] Taken together, the Newt Gingriches, Rush Limbaughs, Pat Robertsons, Kenneth Starrs, Henry Hydes, members of the Religious Right, and other assorted Clinton-haters constituted the most unappealing political opposition since the conservative Republican recalcitrants who bitterly railed against Franklin Roosevelt's New Deal.

As a consequence of talking about virtually nothing else except impeachment for much of Clinton's second term, Republican-style conservatism got a black eye. When asked which party could be trusted to handle the major issues of the day, Democrats took the lead (see

Table 3.1). Even on such issues as handling the economy and managing the federal budget—issues once copyrighted by the Republicans—Democrats surged ahead. As a result, 47 percent wanted the country to continue moving in Clinton's direction; just 29 percent preferred the path outlined by congressional Republicans.[63]

Table 3.1. Issues and Party Images in the 2000 Elections (in percentages)

Issue	Percent Who Say Issue Will Be "Very Important" in 2000 Vote	Democrats	Republicans	Both	Neither	No Opinion
Handling the economy	80	47	42	2	4	5
Managing the federal budget	74	43	40	5	10	2
Protecting the Social Security System	74	52	29	3	8	8
Improving education and the schools	73	51	35	3	6	5
Protecting patients' rights in the health care system	71	53	27	4	9	7

Source: *Washington Post,* "Democrats Have Edge on Election Issues," March 17, 1999, p. A-5. Derived from *Washington Post*/ABC News, survey, March 11–14, 1999.

Given these poor numbers, Republicans turned to popular Texas Governor George W. Bush for help. Bush won a smashing reelection victory in 1998, capturing 69 percent of the vote. His ability to attract traditional Democratic constituencies such as women and Hispanics (who gave him 65 percent and 49 percent of their votes) made him the presumptive favorite to win the GOP presidential nomination in 2000. Bush describes his approach to governance as "inclusive," noting that his administration took the lead in reforming the Texas educational system (including giving poorer school districts more state aid), cutting property taxes, and reducing welfare rolls. Bush's desire to recast the GOP in a more sympathetic light led him to devise the term "compassionate conservatism" to describe his approach to governing. This drew fire from his presidential rivals. Former Education Secretary and Tennessee Governor Lamar Alexander described "compassionate conservatism" as nothing more than "weasel words." Former Vice President Dan Quayle was even more caustic: "I have ordered my staff to never—ever—utter the words 'compassionate conservative.' This silly and insulting term was created by liberal Republicans and is nothing more than code for surrendering our values and principles."[64]

Bush's "compassionate conservatism" was a masterful strategy for wresting the presidency from the Democrats. And while Republican state governors strongly endorse Bush's approach, it is unclear just how long conservative Republicans in Congress will stand for a style that many believe ultimately compromises their ideals and principles. Moreover, Bush's "compassionate conservatism" is not yet firmly rooted in either the party's apparatuses or in the Washington, D.C. think tanks. Republicans may have a charismatic figure in Bush, but what they need is a compelling vision. Simply put, George W. Bush must do what his famous father could not—answer "the vision thing" (a reference to Vice President George Bush's oft-repeated characterization of the barrage of questions he was peppered with concerning what he would do as president). Republicans need to solve this simple mathematical formula: vision=mission. During the four decades of the Cold War, Dwight Eisenhower, Richard Nixon, Barry Goldwater, and Ronald Reagan solved the equation by articulating the place of the United States in the world ("number one"), promising to increase defense spending (which provided many voters with jobs), and promoting American values at home and abroad. Only on the eve of the 2000 elections are Republicans beginning to realize that opposing Clinton is not enough. But their vision remains clouded. For a George W. Bush victory to have much meaning, his administration must include its own Michael Horowitzes who can legitimately claim to have won their handsome offices on the strength of their ideas. Otherwise, Republicans will have power without purpose—a surefire prescription for defeat.

New Democrats, Third Ways, and the Search for True Believers

When Bill Clinton sought the presidency in 1992, the Democratic nomination had become a cheapened commodity. From 1968 to 1988, Democrats had lost five of the previous six contests—a record not equaled since the Republicans lost four times to Franklin Roosevelt and once to Harry Truman. During the glory days of the New Deal, Democrats concocted a formula for surefire victories at the polls: "Big government has something for you." The "gimmes" of the New Deal appealed to a nation where one-third remained "ill-housed, ill-clad, and ill-nourished" (as described by Franklin Roosevelt in his second Inaugural Address). Even when Democrats began routinely losing the presidency after Richard Nixon's 1968 election, Democrats elevated "gimme politics" to an art form in congressional races.

Franklin Roosevelt, Harry Truman, John Kennedy, and Lyndon Johnson transformed a nation of mostly "have-nots" into mostly "haves." But over time, America's new middle class agreed with Republicans like Ronald Reagan that it was the Democrats who loved to "tax and spend, tax and spend." Instead of receiving government services, middle class suburbanites donned the green eye shades of accountants determined to root out any wasteful government spending. Republicans cast their Democratic presidential opponents as profligate spenders who were all too willing to waste valuable taxpayer dollars on dubious programs. This perception became so pervasive that even many *Democrats* had come to view their party negatively. By 1989, only 57 percent had a favorable opinion of their party.[65]

By 1992, Democrats were tired of losing and frantically looking for ways to win. Elaine Ciulla Kamarck and William Galston, two political scientists who were longtime Democratic activists, wrote that a "politics of evasion" had come to dominate Democratic politics. Instead of focusing on ideas, Democrats were enamored with the latest technological advances in fund-raising and poll-taking. By ignoring ideas and values, suburban middle-class families typified by the mythical Nelsons and Cleavers were no longer paying them much heed. To remedy this situation, Kamarck and Galston believed that the 1992 Democratic nominee "must offer a progressive economic message, based on the values of upward mobility and individual effort that can unite the interests of the middle class with those struggling to get there."[66]

This was a tall order, but Bill Clinton was determined to fill it. Having honed his political skills in the wiles of Arkansas politics, Clinton entered the Democratic primaries with these words: "I got into this race because I was tired of Republican neglect and Democratic allegiance to programs that were outmoded. I thought we ought to have a third way."[67] Clinton was not a newcomer to the task of devising new ideas that he could sell to the voters. Back in the late 1970s, Clinton and his poll-taker Dick Morris came to the joint conclusion that American politics was being transformed into a politics of ideas. As Morris later explained:

> I think America fell in love with its politicians in the fifties and sixties when we first saw them on TV. Eisenhower was Dad; Kennedy was handsome; Johnson, our uncle; Nixon the small-town banker. We were innocents. We were newlyweds, and our men could do no wrong. Then came Vietnam, Watergate, lines at gas stations, the bribery scandals of the seventies. Suddenly, our politicians were human beings like us; we became alienated. We got our divorce. We weren't going to be taken in again for a time.
>
> These days, we want to know where a candidate stands—the issues and just the issues. Don't ask us to fall in love; just tell us where you stand, and we'll vote for you. We won't bet our hearts on you, but we'll give you our votes until you screw up.[68]

Following Morris's advice, Clinton began recruiting campaign workers who were motivated by ideas to join him in the grand enterprise of seeking the presidency. To help him reach his lifelong goal of becoming president, Clinton assumed the chairmanship of the Democratic Leadership Council (DLC) in 1990. The DLC was formed five years earlier in the wake of Walter Mondale's landslide defeat. Initially composed of disaffected southerners concerned about maintaining their own elective offices in the wake of the Republican tsunami, the DLC began to reach out to Democrats of all stripes after Michael Dukakis's frustrating loss to George Bush in 1988. DLC Executive Director Al From flew to Little Rock and told Governor Clinton, "Have I got a deal for you." From promised that if Clinton accepted the DLC chairmanship, "We will give you a national platform and I think you will be president of the United States."[69] Immediately, Clinton began using this new venue to position himself as a national leader. In a speech much noticed by the Washington press corps, Clinton told the DLC: "We're here to save the United States of America, not just the Democratic party. Our burden is to give the people a new choice rooted in old values. A new choice that is simple, that offers opportunity, demands responsibility, gives citizens more say, provides them responsive government, all because we recognize that we are community. We're all in this together, and we're going up or down together."[70]

Two years later, Clinton was the Democratic nominee, and thus could dictate much of his party's platform. For the first time, the platform would reflect the "New Democratic" thinking of the Democratic Leadership Council. In a sweeping statement that rejected the New Deal-Great Society nostrums of the past, Clinton promised to find an amalgam of liberal and conservative solutions to the problems besetting the nation:

> We offer a new social contract based neither on callous, do-nothing Republican neglect, nor an outdated faith in programs as the solution to every problem. We favor a Third Way beyond the old approaches—to put government back on the side of citizens who play by the rules. We believe that by what it says and how it conducts its business, government must once again make responsibility an instrument of national purpose. Our future as a nation depends upon the daily assumption of personal responsibility by millions of Americans from all walks of life—for the religious faiths they follow, the ethics they practice, the values they instill, and the pride they take in their work.[71]

Still, many voters remained unpersuaded by the new rhetoric coming from the Democrats. On the eve of the 1992 election, 46 percent described Clinton as a "typical" Democratic presidential candidate; 44 percent saw him as someone who was different from his immediate predecessors.[72] But Clinton remained undaunted. Throughout his presidency, and especially after a poor start in which he seemed more like a New Deal Democrat with a '60s twist (witness health care reform, increased taxes, and gays in the military), Clinton perfected the mantra of the "Third Way." As the Democratic Leadership Council explained it, the Third Way rests on three cornerstones: "The idea that government should promote equal opportunity for all while granting special privilege for none; an ethic of mutual responsibility that equally rejects the politics of entitlement and the politics of social abandonment; and a new approach to governing that empowers citizens to act for themselves."[73]

To achieve these lofty goals, New Democrats proposed new public/private partnerships among individuals, government, and business that would empower ordinary citizens to take charge of their problems and solve them. In particular, Clinton's New Democrats rejected the Darwinian "survival of the fittest" free market extolled by Ronald Reagan and Britain's Margaret Thatcher. Like their New Deal predecessors, Democrats firmly believed that the vagaries of the marketplace and the harsh realities of undiluted capitalism created unacceptable inequities. But they also rejected the Rooseveltian prescription of a big government program designed to solve every problem at hand. As they put it:

> New Progressives seek to replace the old politics of top-down paternalism with a new politics of individual and civic empowerment. Because we can no longer rely on big institutions to take care of us, it is time to craft new policies and new institutions that enable us to take care of ourselves and each other. Ultimately, our challenge is to create a new way of governing that fosters the skills and habits of civic enterprise that have atrophied over the past century of centralization.[74]

A good example of the "Third Way" in action is in Oakland, California. There, the school district was plagued by the large number of area students who wanted more computer usage and training, but lacked the resources to do it. Area businesses were persuaded to give outmoded computers to a new public/private corporation called the Oakland Technology Exchange. Since the fall of 1996, the exchange has received large donations of used computers from area businesses including PeopleSoft, Clorox, and the U.S. Army. Microsoft and IBM donated software licenses. After school, students come to the exchange to refurbish the computers and install new software for a modest wage. In just two years, 3,000 computers have been given to ninety public schools. This innovative use of government, business, and students made everyone a winner: schools got computers, students got vocational education (and a few extra bucks), and area businesses got a trained workforce ready to go to work.[75]

At the local level, public/private partnerships like the Oakland Technology Exchange appeal to a results-oriented electorate. But at the national level, the Third Way lacks much definition. Clinton has continued to follow the advice of his former pollster Dick Morris by focusing on new solutions to old problems. In 1996, for example, Clinton advocated that children wear school uniforms, saying: "As I go around and see what a difference these uniforms make, I think we're really onto something. There are no gang colors, and the girls don't dress in tight clothes. It's a good idea, I'm really getting into it."[76] In an era when children were prone to shoot each other either over a pair of Nike sneakers, or a leather jacket, or just randomly (as in Jonesboro, Arkansas), Clinton's plea for a uniform dress code won widespread approval. To scholars, Clinton's use of the presidential bully pulpit to showcase issues like school uniforms seemed beneath the office that had dealt with the great twentieth century crises of two world wars, a Great Depression, and the cold war. But for disillusioned voters who had met with so many previous disappointments, "show me" and "don't promise more than you can deliver" became important watchwords.

By the completion of his second term, Third Way politics had transformed the presidential wing of the Democratic party. No aspirant for the 2000 nomination seriously challenged Third Way thinking. In fact, heirs to the Old Liberalism that once dominated Democratic politics backed away from challenging Clinton's New Democrats. Particularly noteworthy was Jesse Jackson's decision to take his brand of liberalism out of politics and into the executive suites of corporate America: "These boardrooms, these suites and these offices must be opened up to the light of day. The people that run our companies and who control the allocation of capital in this country must come to understand the value of inclusion. They must not be permitted to act in complete isolation from the values of democracy."[77] The collective decisions of Jackson, Minnesota Senator Paul Wellstone, and House Minority Leader Dick Gephardt not to seek the presidency narrowed the Democratic field to two: Vice President Al Gore and former New Jersey Senator Bill Bradley. Gore, Clinton's designated heir and architect of the New Democrats' "reinventing government" program (a hallmark of Third Way thinking), was so far ahead of any potential rival that only the iconoclastic Bradley dared oppose him. From his perch at the Democratic Leadership Council, a pleased Al From saw a party transformed: "The profound change in the Democratic party is a reality. The Republicans can't win elections any more just by calling Democrats liberals because it's not true. Like the Democrats in the 1980s, the Republicans of the late 1990s have moved out of the mainstream. They've moved off the right side of the road. That's allowed us to occupy the center."[78] In 2000, Clinton and his New Democratic/Third Way politics made the contest a referendum on him that Gore couldn't and didn't lose.

Third Way politics had not only become in vogue in Democratic party circles, but in the old leftist parties of Western Europe. British Prime Minister Tony Blair jettisoned the Labor Party's socialist past and markets what he calls a "New Labor" Party that seeks new solutions to old problems: "We need to have fiscal rectitude and a different role for government as an enabler. We don't need to sit with the old paradigms. I believe we can construct a new and different kind of politics for the 21st century."[79] Blair demolished the Tory opposition in the 1997 elections, amassing a parliamentary majority so large that the Labor advantage actually *exceeds* the total number of Tory seats. One year later, German Social Democratic Party Leader Gerhard Schroeder beat longtime Christian Democrat Chancellor Helmut Kohl. Like Clinton and Blair, Schroeder sought to transform the Social Democratic Party's liberal image along Third Way lines. Italian Prime Minister Romano Prodi is another Third Way protégée.

But the small-deal politics of the Third Way lacks a schema. John Burton, president pro tempore of the California Senate, succinctly summarized the problem: "I don't get this 'New Democrat' b—s. There are only so many ways you can feed hungry people, or get jobs for people who don't have them, and get kids a good education."[80] Rather than an approach, the Third Way is a tactic that allows each of these leaders to say, "We're different." Like most tactics, Third Way politics is hardly inspirational. During his two terms, Clinton has inspired little passion among the Democratic faithful; rather, it is his enemies who have done so. Hatred can be a useful political sword, as Clinton discovered when Kenneth Starr, Newt Gingrich, and Henry Hyde became perfect foils for rallying his fellow Democrats during the impeachment trial. But Clinton's Third Way remains mostly a tactic in search of a rationale. Being different is not enough to create a long-lasting partisan legacy. Woodrow Wilson, for example, was different from his Democratic predecessor Grover Cleveland, yet Wilson was unable to remake the Democratic party into a majority. Most of the advances made by Democrats during the Clinton years have come not as a result of their own strengths, but because the Republicans have been deprived of the ideas that motivated them during the cold war. Thus, as the Clinton era nears its end, it is safe to conclude that the Democratic party has come to a realization that it is as far away from the New Deal as the New Deal was from the Civil War. There can be no going back. The search for ideas—a project conceived by many Democrats as inconceivable in the 1980s—is well under way. But the search is hardly over, and it will be left to others to transform Third Way thinking into a powerful rubric that can be easily understood by policy makers and voters alike.

A Word in Defense of Parties

When actor Robert Redford won his Senate race at the conclusion of the film *The Candidate*, he turned to his political gurus and asked, "Now what do I do?" Echoing Redford, both parties are asking themselves the same question following the inconclusive 2000 presidential contest. The spectacle of Florida county commissioners holding

ballots in the air to detect a pinprick of light is endemic of the proverbial search for the meaning of the election. This essay suggests that
voters did not see much difference between Bush and Gore; indeed,
these two scions of political families were viewed by the vast majority
of Americans as acceptable presidents. Thinking for a moment of the
world of soft drinks, Coke and Pepsi have their fans, but most by-
standers in the cola wars would prefer one about as much as the other.
The same can be said of the Democratic and Republican parties. Their
inability to capture the times and draw distinctions on issues that
voters find relevant does not mean that they are irrelevant. In the
following chapter, Everett Carll Ladd makes a case for *not* strengthening parties (save for the party-in-the-electorate). I disagree. Back in
1942, E. E. Schattschneider argued that the strength of a democracy
rested on the health of its political parties.[81] The weaknesses of the
contemporary party system should make everyone pause. Recall that
Republican David Duke won impressive margins in separate contests
for a Louisiana U.S. Senate seat and later the state governorship despite the intense opposition of the national Republican establishment.
Thankfully, Duke lost. But over the past few decades, demagogues
have appeared on the national stage from *outside the two-party system*.
Alabama Governor George Wallace ran a presidential campaign im-
bued with racist code words as an independent candidate in 1968. In
1992 and again in 1996, Ross Perot won significant public backing—
even though he believed in numerous conspiracies and lacked the
temperament to be president. The demise of the Wallace and Perot
candidacies validates V. O. Key's famous claim that "voters are not
fools."[82]

When parties were stronger, they nominated candidates who represented the broad consensus of American politics and had distinguished careers to boot. Harry Truman and Thomas Dewey are just
two examples of many. Before the presidency, Truman had been a
county judge (commissioner) and a distinguished U.S. Senator who
chaired a congressional committee that exposed excessive and wasteful
spending during World War II. Thomas Dewey had an even more
distinguished career as a U.S. district attorney, special assistant to the
Attorney General, and two-term governor of New York. (Dewey was
elected a third time in 1950.) Both men, like the vast majority of the
nominees who preceded them, were exceptionally well qualified to be

president. But in an era of party weakness, when Democratic and Republican leaders lack the means to control their nominating processes, demagogues have prospered. Few Republican leaders like Pat Buchanan, and most privately view him as an opportunist willing to exploit those left behind in the transition from the Industrial Age to the Information Age. Many Republican leaders view Steve Forbes, Gary Bauer, and Pat Robertson with equal disdain. John McCain appeals to many independents and Democrats, but the GOP establishment finds him to be rigid in his thinking and difficult to work with. The likelihood of any of these candidates being chosen is small, but the thanks is due to the Republican primary electorate (and the charisma of George W. Bush), not because of the opposition of the GOP establishment. Democrats, too, have nominated candidates who have not been well liked by their leadership. Notable among this group was George McGovern, who rankled the Democratic establishment by successfully appealing to the party's most liberal elements. After McGovern lost every state except Massachusetts to Richard Nixon in 1972, Lyndon Johnson liked to tell friends, "I didn't know they made presidential candidates that dumb."[83] Jimmy Carter was different from George McGovern (he won), but he shared McGovern's disdain for the Democratic party hierarchy. Indeed, the lack of any mutual allegiance between Carter and his party mightily contributed to his being a one-term president.

Everett Ladd's claim that being "pro-party" is a normative phrase for being "pro-government" also merits a response. I believe that Ladd correctly notes that the party reformers of the 1950s—especially the authors of *Toward a More Responsible Two-Party System*—wanted government to expand its reach by passing civil rights legislation, reforming health care, giving the newly returning veterans from World War II opportunities like the GI Bill, and seeing to it that the country did not sink into the quagmire of another Great Depression. Ladd quotes E. E. Schattschneider, the chairman of the Committee on Political Parties, as saying: "As a nation we have had little opportunity to prepare ourselves for the realization that *it is now necessary for the government to act as it has never acted before.*"[84]

Certainly, pro-party presidents have used their position to strengthen government. Thomas Jefferson founded the Democratic party, and often railed against excessive government, yet spent the equivalent of one year's worth of the federal budget to make the Louisiana Purchase. Abraham Lincoln abandoned the U.S. Constitution (especially his suspension of habeas corpus) in order to form "a more perfect Union." In so doing, Lincoln remade the Republican party into his instrument for accomplishing this task. Franklin Roosevelt brought two disparate wings of the Democratic party, white southerners and immigrants, together for the New Deal enterprise. None of these presidents were shrinking violets, and all used government to remake their parties into instruments of action. But more recently, Ronald Reagan defied the notion that party reform means a bigger government. The Reagan Revolution was premised on the traditional American values of light governance, individualism, and self-reliance. For the first time, an American president used the shrinking of government to enhance his party's standing. As Reagan told his fellow Republicans in 1984: "A political party isn't a fraternity. It isn't something like the old school tie you wear. You band together in a political party because of certain beliefs of what government should be."[85] Reagan's success is evident in the Clinton era. In his 1996 State of the Union Address, Clinton echoed Reagan's words, saying, "The era of big government is over."[86]

Americans should not be frightened to hear the words "party reform." As our previous two centuries of party government demonstrate, parties are institutions worth having and keeping. The failure of both Democrats and Republicans to energize voters in the post–Cold War era is a *political failure*, not an institutional one. Indeed, the organizational apparatuses of the Democratic and Republican parties have undergone a profound strengthening in recent years. Now if they each could only become a party of ideas.

NOTES

1. *Primary Colors*, 1998 film, Universal Studios.
2. Peter Baker, "Judge Orders Lewinsky to Cooperate," *Washington Post*, 24 January 1999, A-18.
3. Quoted in Caroline Daniel, "Democrats Spend Week Giving Direction to 'Third Way' Ideology," *Washington Post*, 27 September 1998, A-28.
4. Hillary Clinton, interview by Matt Lauer, *Today* NBC, 27 January 1998.

5. Princeton Survey Research Associates for *Newsweek*, survey, 19 February 1999. First question: "We're interested in how your opinion of Mrs. Clinton has changed over the past six years, that is, during the Clinton administration. Has your opinion of Hillary Clinton become more favorable, less favorable, or stayed about the same?" More favorable, 30 percent; less favorable, 14 percent; stayed about the same, 54 percent; don't know, 2 percent. Second question: "Among those who answered 'More favorable' "What is the main reason that your opinion of Mrs. Clinton has become more favorable? Is it because of the way she has supported her husband during recent scandals? The way she has worked for issues you care about? Her strength as a mother? Her political skill?" Supporting her husband, 38 percent; worked for issues you care about, 28 percent; strength as a mother, 11 percent; political skill, 11 percent; other reason (volunteered)/don't know, 12 percent.

6. See Richard L. Berke with Janet Elder, "Damaged by Clinton Trial, Senate Sinks in Public's Eye; GOP is Hurt More," *New York Times*, 3 February 1999, A-1.

7. CBS News/*New York Times*, poll, 26–28 October 1998. Text of questions: "Regardless of how you usually vote, do you think the Republican party or the Democratic party is more likely to make sure the country is prosperous?" Republican, 36 percent; Democratic, 42 percent. Upholding traditional family values: Republican, 47 percent; Democratic, 31 percent. Reduce crime: Republican, 38 percent; Democratic, 31 percent. Cares about people like yourself: Republican, 25 percent; Democratic, 46 percent. Has higher ethical standards: Republican, 41 percent; Democratic, 24 percent. Is more likely to reduce taxes: Republican, 40 percent; Democratic, 40 percent. Has better ideas for leading the country into the twenty-first century: Republican, 33 percent; Democratic, 44 percent. Has more honesty and integrity: Republican, 31 percent; Democratic, 27 percent.

8. Quoted in Berke with Elder, "Damaged by Clinton Trial," A-1.

9. *Newsweek* magazine, post-election poll, 5–6 November 1998. Text of question: "Do you think the two-party system as we know it offers a good range of views and candidates or does it reflect the isolated agenda of the establishment?" Good range of views, 30 percent; reflects establishment, 54 percent.

10. Jesse Ventura, interview by Tim Russert, *Meet the Press* NBC, 8 November 1998.

11. *Newsweek* magazine, post-election poll, 5–6 November 1998. Text of question: "As you may know, former pro wrestler Jesse Ventura was elected governor of Minnesota on Tuesday. Do you think Ventura's election is evidence of a serious trend in the country away from major parties or a fluke that the media is playing up for entertainment purposes?" Evidence of a serious trend, 36 percent; a fluke, 43 percent; don't know, 21 percent.

12. Cited in Martin P. Wattenberg, *The Rise of Candidate-Centered Politics* (Cambridge, Massachusetts: Harvard University Press, 1991), 34.

13. George Washington's Farewell Address, in *Writings of George Washington* (New York: G. P. Putnam and Sons, 1889–93), 223, 225.

14. Alexander Hamilton, "Federalist 68," in Alexander Hamilton, James Madison, and John Jay, *The Federalist Papers* (New York: Mentor Books, 1961), 414.

15. See John Kenneth White, *The New Politics of Old Values* (Hanover, New Hampshire: University Press of New England, 1988), passim.

16. Chilton Research survey for the *Washington Post*/Kaiser Family Foundation/Harvard University, 29 July–18 August 1998. Text of question: "This country would have many fewer problems if there were more emphasis on traditional family values." Agree strongly, 71 percent; agree somewhat, 18 percent; disagree somewhat, 6 percent; disagree strongly, 4 percent.

17. Voter News Service, exit poll, 7 November 2000. Text of question: "Would you like your child to grow up to be president?" Yes, 31 percent; no, 66 percent.

18. Richard A. Gephardt, speech to the John F. Kennedy School of Government, Boston, Massachusetts, 2 December 1997.

19. Richard A. Gephardt, speech on the floor of the House of Representatives, 11 December 1998.

20. James Carville, interview by Tim Russert, *Meet the Press* NBC, 25 January 1998.

21. Quoted in Paul Johnson, *A History of the American People* (New York: HarperCollins, 1997), 937.

22. Quoted in David E. Price, *Bringing Back the Parties* (Washington, DC: Congressional Quarterly, 1984), 100.

23. Quoted in Leon D. Epstein, *Political Parties in the American Mold* (Madison: University of Wisconsin Press, 1986), 18.

24. Committee on Political Parties, *Toward a More Responsible Two-Party System* (New York: Rinehart, 1950), 15.

25. Giovanni Sartori, *Parties and Party System: A Framework for Analysis* (Cambridge, Massachusetts: Harvard University Press, 1976), ix.

26. Everett Carll Ladd, *Where Have All the Voters Gone?* (New York: W.W. Norton, 1982 edition), 70. As will be evident in the subsequent chapter, Ladd has modified his position in the intervening years.

27. "Strengthening the Political Parties," a position paper adopted by the Committee for Party Renewal in 1980 and presented to both national party committees.

28. Testimony of John Kenneth White before the House Task Force on Campaign Finance Reform, Washington, DC, 28 May 1991.

29. For a significant critique of party realignment theory see Everett Carll Ladd, "Like Waiting for Godot: The Uselessness of Realignment of Understanding Change in Contemporary American Politics," *Polity* 22 (Spring 1990): 511–526.

30. See John Kenneth White, *Still Seeing Red: How the Cold War Shapes the New American Politics* (Boulder, Colorado: Westview Press, 1998), passim.

31. Quoted in Richard L. Strout, "Restoring America's Parties," *Christian Science Monitor*, 25 September 1977, 31.

32. Ralph M. Goldman, "Who Speaks for the Political Parties or, Martin Van Buren, Where Are You When We Need You?" in John C. Green and Daniel M. Shea, eds., *The State of the Parties* (Lanham, Maryland: Rowman and Littlefield Publishers, 1996), 25–41.

33. See Epstein, *Political Parties in the American Mold,* especially 155–199.

34. Antonin Scalia, dissent, *Tashjian v. Republican Party of Connecticut,* in *Supreme Court Reporter* (1986), 560–561.

35. See *Eu v. San Francisco County Democratic Central Committee,* in *Supreme Court Reporter* (1989), 1021. The vote in this case was 8-0. Chief Justice William Rehnquist did not participate.

36. *Colorado Republican Federal Campaign Committee and Douglas Jones, Treasurer, Petitioners v. Federal Election Commission,* 1996 U.S. Lexis-Nexis, 8.

37. See Justice Thomas's concurring opinion in *Colorado Republican Federal Campaign Committee and Douglas Jones, Treasurer, Petitioners v. Federal Election Commission,* 1996 U.S. Lexis-Nexis, 21.

38. *Rutan, et al. v. Republican Party of Illinois* (1990), 1, 11.

39. Ibid., 15.

40. George McGovern, *Grassroots: The Autobiography of George McGovern* (New York: Random House, 1977), 137.

41. *Mandate for Reform: A Report of the Commission on Party Structure and Delegate Selection to the Democratic National Committee* (Washington, DC: April 1970).

42. See Thomas Cronin and Robert Loevy, "The Case for a National Pre-Primary Convention," *Public Opinion* (December/January 1983): 50–53; Martin P. Wattenberg, "When You Can't Beat Them, Join Them: Shaping the Presidential Nominating Process to the Television Age," *Polity* 21 (Summer 1989): 587–597; Gerald M. Pomper, "Primaries *After* Conventions," *New York Times,* 2 January 1988, 23; Gary L. Rose, ed., *Controversial Issues in Presidential Selection* (Albany: State University of New York Press, 1991), 287–289.

43. For more information on this, see John Kenneth White and Jerome M. Mileur, "Where Angels Fear to Tread: Toward a Larger National Role in a Federal System of Presidential Nomination" (paper presented at the annual meeting of the Midwest Political Science Association, Chicago, IL April 1989).

44. Al Gore had a popular vote plurality of 337,576 over George W. Bush. But Bush won 271 electoral votes to Gore's 267.

45. Others have proposed more radical solutions. James MacGregor Burns favors a "team ticket" where presidential and congressional candidates would run together. See James MacGregor Burns, *The Power to Lead* (New York: Simon and Schuster, 1984), 199–202. Burns would impose a parliamentary system upon the existing Constitution—something most Americans strongly reject.

46. President Ford Committee, "Ford Campaign Strategy Plan," August 1976. Courtesy of Gerald R. Ford Library.

47. See especially Jerome M. Mileur, "Massachusetts: The Democratic Party Charter Movement," in Gerald M. Pomper, ed., *Party Renewal in America* (New York: Praeger, 1980), 159–175.

48. This was Lieutenant Governor Thomas P. O'Neill III (son of the late House Speaker). Many thought O'Neill's presence would have taken votes away from Dukakis.

49. See John Kenneth White, testimony before the House Task Force on Campaign Finance Reform, 28 May 1991.

50. The story is told in E. J. Dionne, Jr., "Catholics and the Democratic Estrangement but not Desertion" in Seymour Martin Lipset, ed., *Party Coalitions in the 1980s* (San Francisco: Institute for Contemporary Studies, 1981), 308.

51. "Boston Gives Heart to Smith: Greeting Breaks All Records," *Boston Evening Globe*, 24 October 1928, 1.

52. Alfred E. Smith, *Up to Now: An Autobiography* (New York: Viking Press, 1929), 403.

53. Gregg Easterbrook, "Ideas Move Nations," *Atlantic Monthly*, January 1986, 80.

54. Quoted in Arthur M. Schlesinger, Jr., *The Vital Center* (Boston: Houghton Mifflin, 1949), 17.

55. See White, *Still Seeing Red*, especially 79–150.

56. Richard M. Nixon, *Beyond Peace* (New York: Random House, 1994), 8.

57. *Washington Post*/ABC News, survey, 11–14 March 1999. Text of question: "Which political party, the Democrats or the Republicans, do you trust to do a better job [of] encouraging high moral standards and values?" Democrats, 30 percent; Republicans, 43 percent; both equally, 5 percent; neither, 17 percent; don't know, 5 percent. Interestingly, Democrats had the edge when respondents were asked, "Which party better represents your own personal values?" Democrats, 47 percent; Republicans, 39 percent; both equally, 3 percent; neither, 8 percent; don't know, 3 percent.

58. George Hager, "GOP Tax-Cutting Budget Plans Open Double-Barrel Hill Debate," *Washington Post*, 18 March 1999, A-4.

59. *Washington Post*/ABC News, survey, 11–14 March 1999.

60. Cited in Lydia Saad, "GOP Image Losing Its Luster," *The Polling Report*, 30 November 1998, 1.

61. Gallup/CNN/*USA Today* poll, 18–19 March 1998. Text of questions: "Should Kenneth Starr end his investigation and give the results to Congress?" Yes, 60 percent; no, 34 percent. "Is Kenneth Starr going too far?" Yes, 58 percent; no, 37 percent.

62. Quoted in Bob Woodward and Peter Baker, "Behind Calm Air, President Hides Rage Over Starr," *Washington Post*, 1 March 1998, A-1.

63. *Washington Post*/ABC News, poll, 11–14 March 1999. Text of question: "Do you think the country should go in the direction President Clinton wants to lead it, go in the direction the Republicans in Congress want to lead

it, or what?" Clinton's direction, 47 percent; Republicans' direction, 29 percent; no difference/no opinion, 11 percent; neither direction, 7 percent; other direction, 6 percent.

64. Quoted in E.J. Dionne, Jr., "Construction Boon: It's No Accident That the GOP Is Being Rebuilt by Its Governors," *Washington Post*, 14 March 1999, B-4.

65. Cited in William Galston and Elaine Ciulla Kamarck, *The Politics of Evasion: Democrats and the Presidency* (Washington, DC: The Progressive Policy Institute, September 1989), 1.

66. Ibid., 27.

67. Quoted in Jonathan Chait, "The Slippery Center," *The New Republic*, 16 November 1998, 19.

68. Dick Morris, *Behind the Oval Office: Winning the Presidency in the Nineties* (New York: Random House, 1997), 47.

69. Chait, "The Slippery Center," 19.

70. David Maraniss, *First in His Class* (New York: Simon and Schuster, 1995), 459.

71. *The Democratic Party Platform* (Washington, DC: Democratic National Committee, 1992), 7.

72. CBS News/*New York Times*, survey, 31 October–1 November 1992. Text of question: "Do you think Bill Clinton and Al Gore are different from Democratic presidential candidates in previous years, or are they typical Democratic candidates?" Different, 44 percent; typical, 46 percent; both (volunteered), 2 percent; don't know/no answer, 9 percent.

73. "The New Progressive Declaration: A Political Philosophy for the Information Age," *The New Democrat*, 10 July 1996.

74. Ibid.

75. "Idea of the Week: Recycling Computers for Schools," in *The DLC Update*, 18 September 1998.

76. Morris, *Behind the Oval Office*, 227.

77. Statement of Jesse L. Jackson, Sr., press release, 24 March 1999.

78. Quoted in William Schneider, "No Modesty Please, We're the DLC," *National Journal*, 12 December 1998.

79. Quoted in Daniel, "Democrats Spend Week Giving Direction to 'Third Way' Ideology." See also Tony Blair, *New Britain: My Vision of a Young Country* (Boulder, Colorado: Westview Press, 1997).

80. Quoted in Mark Shields, "California's Comeback Kid," *Washington Post*, 22 March 1998, C-11.

81. E. E. Schattschneider, *Party Government* (New York: Rinehart, 1942), 1.

82. V. O. Key, *The Responsible Electorate: Rationality in Presidential Voting, 1936–1962* (New York: Vintage Books, 1966), 7.

83. Quoted in Merle Miller, *Lyndon: An Oral Biography* (New York: Ballantine Books, 1980), 673.

84. E. E. Schattschneider, *The Struggle for Party Government* (College Park, Maryland: Program in American Civilization, University of Maryland, 1948), 1.

85. Hugh Sidey, "A Conversation with Reagan," *Time*, 3 September 1984.

86. Bill Clinton, State of the Union Address, Washington, DC, 23 January 1996.

4

On the Need for Parties "Strong" and "Great": A Dissent

EVERETT CARLL LADD

For most of this century, political science orthodoxy has held that American political parties need strengthening, to the end of improving the quality of the nation's democracy. In his essay in this volume, John Kenneth White (see chapter 3) highlights some of the key documents in the orthodoxy's unfolding. E. E. Schattschneider gave the case eloquent expression in *Party Government*. A few years later, Professor Schattschneider reentered the fray as chair of the American Political Science Association's Committee on Political Parties. The result was a report, less analytical than normative: *Toward a More Responsible Two-Party System*. For the last twenty years, the Committee for Party Renewal, in which White has been an active member and spokesman, has carried high the torch for stronger parties. "Without parties there can be no organized and coherent politics," the Committee expounded in a "Statement of Principles," a position paper it adopted in September 1976 and reaffirmed in 1980. "Parties are indispensable to the realization of democracy. The stakes are no less than that."

Reflecting faithfully the position of the Committee for Party Renewal and the longtime political science backing for "more responsible" political parties, White insists that the party system needs to be strengthened in all its forms. Party organization must be revitalized and refurbished. Political parties need to be more coherent and programmatic actors throughout government decision making. And, the ties of individual voters to political parties need to be made deeper and more determinative of voting decisions. In this view, a bigger party presence is the sine qua non of improved governmental performance, and thus of restored citizen confidence in the political system.

I've been dissatisfied with this political science orthodoxy—and increasingly so. For a time in a somewhat foolish youth, I embraced the notion that stronger parties would mean stronger democracy. As my thinking matured, however, I came to see the argument as resting primarily on a normative rather than an empirical base. Political science was in fact offering a statement of desired ends with regard to government's role in public life, far more than analysis of the kind of party role effective democracy requires. I expressed my dissatisfaction in earlier works—including a chapter in a book by White in 1992, and more fully in an article published in the *Political Science Quarterly* in 1987. I now believe that my earlier essays were too kind to the "responsible party" position.

TOCQUEVILLE AND "GREAT PARTIES"

Political scientists advocating stronger parties have often found comfort in the commentary of Alexis de Tocqueville. The great Frenchman's standing is high in American social science generally—and nowhere higher than in the assessment of the present authors. If Tocqueville endorsed stronger parties, then, the goal has an impressive ally.

Tocqueville did not deal with the strength of voter ties to parties or the internal discipline of parties in government. But he did seem to come down on the side of an enlarged party presence in his discussion of "great" and "minor," or "small," parties. He wrote in the first volume of *Democracy in America*:

> The political parties that I style great are those which cling to principles rather than to their consequences; to general and not to special cases; to ideas and not to men. These parties are usually distinguished by nobler features, more generous passions, more genuine convictions, and a more bold and open conduct than the others. In them, private interest, which always plays the chief part in political passions is more studiously veiled under the pretext of the public good.

Great parties are, then, ones with a larger reach in ideas and principles that contend with one another to determine fundamental direction of a polity. The Washington-Adams-Hamilton Federalists were, in Tocqueville's view, a great party, as were Jefferson's Republicans. Tocqueville saw America's founding as a time of national greatness.

In contrast, the America of Andrew Jackson's presidency, which Tocqueville visited, had, in the Frenchman's view, only "small" parties. "[I]t happens that when a calm state succeeds a violent revolution," he wrote, "great men seem suddenly to disappear and the powers of the human mind to lie concealed." He paints a rather despairing picture of small parties.

> [They] are generally deficient in political good faith. As they are not sustained or dignified by lofty purposes, they ostensibly display the selfishness of their character in their actions. They glow with a factitious zeal; their language is vehement, but their conduct is timid and irresolute. The means which they employ are as wretched as the end at which they aim.

It's easy to see what Tocqueville had in mind by these references. The party activity he witnessed in the 1830s often seemed petty. It involved a highly developed interest in patronage, but often failed to climb to loftier aims. It was a time of consummate party "wheeler-dealers" such as Martin Van Buren, who was Jackson's vice president and then for a term president himself (1837–41). It was a time when "party bosses" made their appearance on our political stage. The reach of the conflict between the "Jackson men" and the "Adams men," and, later, that between the Democrats and the Whigs, seemed to Tocqueville petty in comparison to the struggle between the Federalists and the Anti-federalists over the institutional future of the American Revolution—and so, of course, it was.

Great intuitive thinker that he was, Tocqueville recognized a flaw in his own reasoning and preferences, however, which led him to qualify his initial distinction. "*Society is convulsed by great parties,*" he continued, but "*it is only agitated by minor ones; it is torn by the former,* by the *latter it is [only] degraded* (. . . America has had great parties, but has them no longer; and if) *her happiness is thereby considerably increased,* her *morality has suffered.*" [Emphasis added.]

Narrow, often self-serving patronage parties are not an ideal many of us wish to defend, and Tocqueville certainly did not defend them. Still, he felt compelled to argue that the absence of great parties in the America of the 1830s meant that the nation's "happiness is thereby considerably increased." And, seeing much to commend in the earlier American experience with great parties, he felt obliged to observe nonetheless that society in general "is convulsed" by them. Whatever was he talking about?

Just this. There is real splendor in seeing a party of large reach and high principle do battle in a time of great transition in a polity. The spectacle is all the more attractive, naturally, if that truly great party wins. Tocqueville's European experience made him keenly aware, of course, that it was by no means certain it would win. A party of expansive support but debased of principle could well triumph.

Beyond this, nineteenth-century liberal that he was, Tocqueville recognized that having people consumed by politics is not a proper long-run goal for the polity. There will be times when the citizenry must be so absorbed, and one devoutly hopes the parties of that day will serve them well in their search for better government. But much of the time a more prosaic existence has its attractions. This is what Tocqueville meant when he said that a kind of normalization of politics in Jacksonian America contributed and attested to the happiness of the people. A less "politicized" environment has its virtues—in contentment if not grandeur.

STRONG PARTIES—AND STRONG GOVERNMENT

The argument that the United States needs "more" by way of political parties rests, I've argued, on a bundle of normative assumptions bearing on what government should do, not on inherent democratic requirements. It goes hand in hand with several other arguments: (1) that the United States needs more government programs to "solve national problems"; (2) that the separation of powers/checks-and-balances system that lies at the heart of the American experiment with political institutions is a terrible barrier to getting needed programs enacted; and (3) that a *good society* requires a *big polity*.

A good example of this point is found in E. E. Schattschneider whose argument about parties was at its core a call for a larger state. This fact is never clearer than in his 1948 work, *The Struggle for Party Government.*

> As a nation we have had little opportunity to prepare our-selves for the realization that it is now necessary for the gov-ernment to act as it has never acted before. . . . The essence of the governmental crisis consists of a deficiency of the power to create, adopt, and execute, a comprehensive plan of action in advance of a predictable catastrophe in time to prevent and minimize it. . . . The central difficulty of the whole system—the difficulty which causes all of the difficulties—is the fact that the government characteristically suffers from a deficiency of the power to govern.

Schattschneider had every right to express his own normative point of view. It's not hard to see how he arrived at the following prescription, in effect saying: "I think we need more government to advance interests which I believe are insufficiently assisted at present. And, I see the need for a well-disciplined, programmatic political party to advance this end. If such a party can win a majority in Congress and capture the White House, it can override separation of powers restraints and legislate boldly. Until and unless we get such a party (and hence party system), we're destined to live through long periods when government's programmatic reach is curbed—this condition broken only by brief intervals when a great crisis, like the Great Depression, opens the door to decisive action."

Many political scientists are generally comfortable with this nor-mative position. Here, we have no interest in entering an extended normative dispute. That's not the present volume's purpose. Never-theless, our argument is that none of the core assumptions—that more government means a more effective democracy, separation of powers is antiquated, and a relatively large polity is generally good for society—rests on an empirical foundation. These ideas are hopes and value judgments, not the work of a science of politics.

It *is* likely that stronger, more disciplined parties would result in more governmental action. It's not by chance that the United States, where political parties are institutionally weaker than in any other industrial democracy, is also the country where the reach of the national government is—though it has expanded greatly in recent decades—the most restricted still. More collectivist, less individualist political outlooks encourage the formation of stronger, more elite-directed parties, and such parties are in turn powerful instruments for state action. Granted, party discipline may on occasion be used, as it was in part in Margaret Thatcher's Britain, to dismantle programs enacted by earlier governments, Labour and Conservative alike. But on the whole, one wants strong parties in order to advance "positive" government—to enact and enlarge programs.

While the proposition has rarely been subject to systematic empirical examination, some political scientists have at least questioned whether strong parties have in fact been associated with sound public policy. Leon D. Epstein has observed, for instance, that both Don K. Price and Pendleton Herring concluded at the end of the Depression decade that the disciplined party leadership found in the United Kingdom might well have produced far less desirable policy results than the United States' relatively weak and decentralized parties operating in a system of vastly separated and checked authority. Whether strong parties tend to advance sounder policy is, admittedly, a huge and complex empirical question. But until it is seen as an empirical question, treatment of it can't advance much beyond the position, "Well, that's what I want anyway!" We can find little in the canon of American political science that gives more empirical weight to the critics of the present workings of separation of powers then to its proponents. Evidence seems at least as strong for the argument that America's sweeping system of separated power, relatively uncurbed by "strong" and "great" parties, has improved public policy by helping slow the rush of government expansion and lessen the likelihood of ill-considered, precipitant action.

Questioning the Ideal of "Maximalist Politics"

The idea that "more politics" is more or less automatically desirable is deeply entrenched in contemporary political commentary—in the writings of political scientists, journalists, and other commentators.

We see this in the literature on nonvoting. With some notable exceptions, much of the work on voter turnout sees low turnout as a huge problem, as a failure of the polity. I certainly don't advocate low voter participation. Everyone should have a full and unimpeded right to vote in this and any other country that claims to be democratic, and everyone should be encouraged, we believe, to exercise his or her rights as a citizen to select political leadership. There can never be too much education on behalf of the responsibilities and the opportunities of vigorous citizenship—which surely must include turning out to vote regularly.

One may insist on the above, however, without subscribing to the argument that the relatively low turnout in the United States— about 54% of the adult resident population casting votes for president in 1996, for example—is on its face evidence of a grievous weakness in our democratic life. But many have argued that it does indicate just that. Thus Arthur T. Hadley wrote:

> America's present problem . . . is an apathetic, cross-pressured society with strong feelings of political impotence, where more and more people find their lives out of control, believe in luck, and refrain from voting. These growing numbers of refrainers hang over our democratic process like a bomb, ready to explode and change the course of our history. . . . For us, now, an increase in voting is a sign of political health.

Gary R. Orren argues that "if the health of a democracy can be measured by the level of popular participation in its electoral system, ours is ailing." Graham Allison asks, rhetorically, "When half the people drop out, what does this imply about the legitimacy of a democratic government . . . ?" The list of such commentary goes on and on.

The argument is riddled with flaws. Consider, for example, Hadley's view that America is beset by an increasing, widespread decline of social obligation and participation—a surge in the number of "refrainers." This is simply not true. It is the case that voter turnout has declined some from the 1960 level—the highest in this century. But turnout in the 1990s was almost exactly what it was in 1936— a presidential election year in which Franklin Roosevelt and the New Deal had presumably galvanized the population to action. As political scientist Peter Bruce has shown, voter turnout in 1996 was in fact two percentage points higher than it was in 1988. Moreover, outside the arena of voting rates, the data decisively refute the argument that participation is in decline. A major study done in 1990 under the direction of Sidney Verba and his colleagues showed, once again, a populace that is highly participatory in most areas of political activity (such as contributing money to political organizations, getting in contact with government officials, and the like) and even more so in nonpolitical public affairs (from a vast variety of organizational memberships to charitable giving and voluntary action).

Similarly, I've shown that, far from declining, charitable giving and voluntary action levels are increasing in the United States, and that the level of U.S. participation dwarfs that in western Europe. Table 4.1 provides data showing clearly how unfounded is the claim that America is a nation of "refrainers."

Table 4.1. Volunteering and Giving: Again the U.S. is Different

Volunteering and Giving	U.S.	Germany	France
Respondents who volunteered during previous twelve months	49%	13%	19%
Respondents who contributed during previous twelve months	73%	44%	43%
Average sum of donation for previous twelve months for givers	$851	$120	$96

Source: Survey by the Gallup Organization (U.S.) for the Independent Sector, latest that of 1991; Zentrum fuer Umfragen, Methoden und Analysen & Gesellschaft fuer Marketing-Kommunikations-und Sozialforschung mbH (Germany), 1992; and I.L.S. Survey for Laboratoire D'Ëconomie Sociale and the Fondation de France (France), 1991.

Returning to the matter of voter turnout as such, many different factors account for the American experience of relatively low participation. Not all of these are causes for concern. Ivor Crewe notes, for example, that while turnout in a given national election in the United States falls below that in western Europe, Americans vote in far more contests than Europeans do. We vote for municipal and state officials, as well as national government officeholders. At the local level we vote separately in a variety of overlapping jurisdictions—cities and counties, school districts, sanitation districts, and so forth. And, of course, we vote in elections that choose party nominees (primaries) as well as those which choose among party candidates. In all, Crewe notes, Americans are asked to go to the polls far more often than the citizens of any other democracy. Not surprisingly, no one election is anything of a novelty. The frequency of our elections probably reduces the turnout in any one.

Some factors that encourage high turnout are highly undesirable. It seems clear, for example, that extreme fear about electoral outcomes can be a powerful incentive to vote—so as to prevent, hopefully, the feared outcome. Columnist George F. Will has reminded us that in the two presidential ballots conducted in Germany in 1932, 86 percent and 84 percent of the electorate cast ballots. In 1933, 89 percent voted in the assembly election in which the Nazis triumphed. Will asked: "Did the high 1933 turnout make the Nazi regime especially legitimate? Were the 1932 turnouts a sign of the health of the Weimar Republic?" His answer is the right one: "The turnouts reflected the unhealthy stakes of politics then: elections determined which mobs ruled the streets and who went to concentration camps."

In less dramatic cases, too, the degree of stability of a country's democratic government influences the voting rates. Thus, turnout has been higher in Germany—a country that experienced great political turmoil and instability up until the end of World War II, than in Great Britain, where democracy has been relatively tranquil for well over a century. What's more, participation rates have tended to decline in Europe since World War II. Participation declined from the late 1940s to the present in western Germany, for example, and in France—although it's still higher in both these countries than it is in the United States. The United States is the world's oldest democracy—the one country where contested free elections have been held continuously since the latter years of the eighteenth century. The states that remained in the Union even held a highly contested vote for president in 1864, in the midst of the Civil War. Of course, Americans are less inclined to fear massive upheaval or a dramatic discontinuity resulting from any particular election. In this environment, some people who are less interested in politics apparently feel a degree of security sufficient to permit them *not to vote*.

Again, I trust readers will recognize I'm not writing "in defense of nonvoting." My argument instead is that "more politics" is not automatically a good thing, that a condition in which many people feel free to concentrate their energies on other aspects of lives—raising families, working in churches, volunteering their time to help invalids, or giving money to charitable institutions—has much to commend it. If better citizenship education and changes in electoral processes can help more people vote as well, so much the good. Let's do it. But let's not claim that relatively low voter turnout is necessarily a sign of an apathetic populace generally abandoning its common and collective responsibilities.

The American ideological tradition has, from the country's forming, insisted on the need for a *large public sector* and a relatively *small state*. The American idea has been that our common or public concerns as a people require vigorous activity outside the sphere of government. Tocqueville remarked on this point at length a century and a half ago. He noted, for example, the extraordinary interest-group activity on behalf of all kinds of issues and objectives.

> The political associations that exist in the United States are only a single feature in the midst of the immense assemblage of associations in that country. Americans of all ages, all conditions, and all dispositions constantly form associations. . . . The Americans make associations to give entertainments, to found seminaries, to build inns, to construct churches, to diffuse books, to send missionaries to the antipodes; in this manner they found hospitals, prisons, and schools. . . . Wherever at the head of some new undertaking you see the government in France, or a man of rank in England, in the United States you will be sure to find an association.

In the first volume to the *Democracy*, written five years earlier, Tocqueville had given the classic statement of the fact that—far from holding back collective energy and participation—American individualism was its very source: "In the United States associations are established to promote the public safety, commerce, industry, morality, and religion. There is no end which the human will despair of attaining through the combined power of individuals united into a society."

TODAY'S PUBLIC ASSESS GOVERNMENT

Over the last several decades, Americans have been expressing increasingly ambivalent feelings about the scope of government and the quality of governmental performance. I have reviewed these data at length in an ongoing series of articles and data compilations in the pages of *Public Opinion, The American Enterprise, The Public Perspective,* and other publications.

On the one hand, Americans have remained, despite their complaints about government's record, an optimistic people who believe that problems are something to be solved, not endured. Thus, in an age of considerable national affluence, we have fairly high expectations with regard to action, in areas as wide ranging as the environment, crime, schools, healthcare, and poverty. We want action in these areas and usually see governmental action as one part of the necessary response.

On the other hand, all kinds of indicators reveal doubts about the wisdom of continuing to expand government's reach. Ever since the passage of Proposition 13 in California in 1978, tax protests have been a common part of the American political experience, and a highly democratic one at that. That is, the strongest insistence that tax hikes be curbed has often come from the lower half of the income spectrum, not from the upper half. In general, Americans have endorsed major interventions by government, and yet at the same time have called government too big, too inefficient, too intrusive. Given the choice between government which does more and costs more, and that which does less and costs less, Americans are indicating strong preference for the latter. The data in figures 4.1 and 4.2 attest to this "bottom-line" judgment.

Figure 4.1. Government: Yes to Less

Question: Which of the following statements do you agree with more: I'd rather pay higher taxes to support a larger government that provides more services, or I'd rather pay lower taxes and have a smaller government that provides fewer services?

Question: When it comes to the current size of the federal government, which statement comes closer to your view—the federal government is too big, the federal government is about the right size, or the federal government has been cut too much?

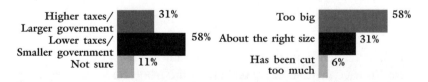

Higher taxes/ Larger government — 31%
Lower taxes/ Smaller government — 58%
Not sure — 11%

Too big — 58%
About the right size — 31%
Has been cut too much — 6%

Source: Survey by Opinion Dynamics for Fox News, June 11–12, 1997

Source: Survey by the Gallup Organization for CNN/*USA Today,* January 6–7, 1998.

Figure 4.2 Government: At Least, The Answer Isn't More

Question: Some people think the government is trying to do too many things that should be left to individuals and businesses. Others think that government should do more to solve our contry's problems. Which comes closer to your own view?

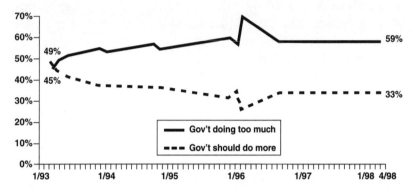

Source: Surveys by Gallup/CNN/*USA Today*, March 22–24, 1993, April 22–24, 1993, April 17–19, 1998; Yankelovich Partners/Time/CNN, June 17–21, 1993, February 24–27, 1996, September 12–17, 1996; Gallup/CNN/ *USA Today,* December 17–19, 1993, January 15–17, 1994, October 22–25, 1994, November 2–26, 1994, December 15–18, 1995, January 12–15, 1996.

The founders of the American system sought to establish and sustain a type of government at once energetic and limited. This admixture of seeming opposites is in one sense jarring, but it has received the continuing support of much of the populace. The levels of government today are far higher than they were in the past, but the same admixture obtains. The American system continues to produce government that is extraordinarily energetic and highly constrained.

We Don't Need a More Activist Party System

If Americans are ambivalent about government's proper role and reluctant to issue the call, "Charge!" and if they show no signs of wanting to strengthen political parties, why should we urge upon them steps toward a stronger and "more responsible" party system? The only defensible answer would be because, though much of the public doesn't know it, the absence of a stronger party system is a major reason why so many people are so dissatisfied with governmental performance. Is that answer valid?

One reason to doubt its validity is the fact that dissatisfaction with government's performance is evident in nearly all of the world's industrial democracies, not just the United States. Indeed, the United States does not rank at all high comparatively on many of these measures compared to other countries. If many countries with strong party systems manifest as much or more dissatisfaction with governmental institutions and performance as the U.S. does, the idea that strengthening our party system is likely to contribute to increased satisfaction and confidence is dubious at best.

The argument on behalf of stronger parties needs to be examined in the three distinct arenas in the party literature—party in the electorate, party organization, and party in government. The case for stronger parties in the latter two seems to us very weak. What's more, the argument runs in precisely the opposite direction from what the public says it wants. The public's criticism, as seen clearly in survey data, is that politics is too much captured by political insiders—e.g., by the elected Democratic and Republican politicians in the national legislature—and in general that "the system" is too insulated from meaningful, day-to-day popular control. The call is to somehow check and limit the "political class."

The last thing this public wants is stronger party organization and stronger party apparatus in government. Its present discontents push it in a direction similar to that pursued by the Progressive movement early in this century. The Progressives believed that the principal institutions of American representative democracy—political parties, legislatures, city councils, and the like—had been captured by "the interests," were riddled with corruption, and often had been wrested from popular control. Muckraking journalists, among them Ida M. Tarbell and Lincoln Steffens, graphically portrayed the venality and unresponsiveness that they saw as all too common in the nation's political life. Finley Peter Dunne, a popular American humorist, was a friend of many of the muckrakers. Dunne had his famous character, Mr. Dooley, tell his friend Hinnissy that he had once enjoyed reading newspapers and magazines, but no more:

"... What do I find? Everything has gone wrong.... Is there an honest man among us? If there is, throw him out. He's a spy. Is there an institution that isn't corrupt to its very foundation? Don't ye believe it. It only looks that way because our graft iditor hasn't got there on his rounds yet."

Many in the Progressive movement concluded that the only way to cure these ills was to give individual citizens new authority to override and control representative institutions. They backed and saw enacted a host of "direct democracy" reforms: the direct primary, to take nominations away from party "bosses"; initiatives and referenda, to allow the people to make laws directly; and the recall, to permit voters to "kick the bums out"—if their performance was objectionable—even before their regular terms were up. The success of the reformers makes clear that they tapped a deep lode of resentment.

Today too the public is evidently angry about the performance of its political institutions. What's more, current frustrations resemble those of the Progressive era and probably surpass anything in between that era and our own. As in the Progressive era, dissatisfaction gets expressed in increased backing for direct democracy. The American political culture is strongly individualist, and we are always sympathetic to the idea of direct citizenry intervention above and beyond elections. But when things are seen going poorly in terms of the institutions' performance, direct democracy's appeal gets a special boost.

Many of the innovations of the Progressive era, such as referenda and primaries, are in wide use. The public would extend them further now. But today's direct democracy agenda finds other expressions. Backing for term limits is one. If legislators are unresponsive, limit the number of years they can serve. Surveys in various states and those taken nationally have shown overwhelming backing for this idea. Every time the public has had a chance to vote on them it has endorsed term limits. The Perot movement was yet another expression. So was Jesse Ventura's victory on the Reform Party line in Minnesota in 1998. The public has expressed general dissatisfaction with "politics as usual."

Political science has long favored a strengthening of parties, as opposed to more direct democracy, as the answer to governmental unresponsiveness and as the means for increasing popular control. The public plainly doesn't agree. Some might dismiss its evident disagreement with anything that smacks of augmenting party apparatus and control as simply the unthinking excesses of a highly individualist culture. The culture is highly individualist, and that is not going to change, so practical politics suggests the need to make improvements within its dictates. But beyond this, if Americans are at times excessively obedient to individualist assertions, it's not at all clear that they are wrong on the proper role of party organization and party machinery in government. Party leaders are political insiders. As modern government has expanded so profoundly, the political class has become more insulated. Finding ways to further check it might permit ordinary voters to intervene more effectively and extensively in setting public policy.

There is reason to question these assumptions. The United States is not beset by the old-fashioned venality and corruption that the Progressives faced, but the primary representative institutions often seem worlds apart from the general public, responding to insider agendas. Politics as usual "inside the beltway" is highly insulated and in a sense isolated. The interests that dominate "beltway politics" differ from those the Progressives battled, but they may be no less insensitive to popular calls for change. The old Progressive answer of extending direct citizenry authority and intervention deserves careful reconsideration as a part of the answer to present-day insufficiencies and shortcomings in representative democracy.

Maybe We Should Have a Little More Party Organization of the Electorate

The one area where we see a strong case for modest steps to strengthen the party presence involves party in the electorate. One of the most unusual features of the contemporary party system is the frequency with which split results are attained—for example, the Republicans winning the presidency pretty regularly, while not since 1954 having control of both houses of Congress. This condition seems to have two quite different sources: one involving something that much of the public intends, but the other quite unintentional and indeed fundamentally unwanted.

The "intended" dimension, which I discussed in terms of "cognitive Madisonianism," starts from the evident fact that Americans are from their history less likely than their counterparts in other democ-racies to be troubled about divided control. It accords with the gen-eral thrust and biases of separation of powers. Into this, it seems, something new has been added. The high measure of ambivalence that so many citizens have about government's role, and from there the doubts they entertain about both political parties, seem to be well served or expressed by electoral outcomes which, frequently, give each of the major parties a piece of the action.

Today's public wants somewhat contradictory things of the modern state, and it sees the Democrats and Republicans as differing significantly on the issue of government's role. Given this, a kind of "cognitive Madisonianism" seems to have emerged—insisting that the two parties' competing views on government's proper role be pitted one against another, as when a Republican executive pushes one way and a Demo-cratic legislature the other. The empirical work needed to explore cog-nitive Madisonianism satisfactorily has not been done, despite extensive surveys on related topics. We do know that high degrees of ambivalence concerning government's role have been present over the last several decades, but that survey data show nothing comparable for earlier periods. We also know that large segments of the public—usually solid majori-ties—express broad approval of divided government.

Those who see evidence of cognitive Madisonianism in the two-tier voting must acknowledge nonetheless that more is at work. Even in the face of pronounced voter dissatisfaction with Congress, for example, historically unprecedented majorities of incumbents of both parties have been winning reelection, and House of Representative incumbents typically win by big margins. Underlying this develop-ment are several notable features of contemporary electioneering: (1) incumbents generally enjoy huge advantages in campaign contribu-tions; (2) they also enjoy a big advantage in government-provided resources—notably in the very large staffs given members through the "reforms" of the late 1960s and early 1970s; and (3) in races for governor and senator, as well as that for president, many voters lack information on the policy stands of House members. Instead, they are likely to have some vaguely favorable image of him or her, while having no impression at all of the challenger.

Getting voters to pay a bit more attention to party labels is the one thing that could upset this present dynamic. A voter might not know anything about a member of Congress's voting record but still vote against him or her in favor of a challenger who is less known because the voter wanted to change party control, to give the "outs" a chance. Evidence abounds to show that this is exactly what has happened historically. Over the last several decades, however, as incumbents have gained election resources far greater than ever before, the proportion of voters bound by significant "party awareness" has declined precipitously. "Vote for the person, not the party," is in many ways laudable. It conforms entirely to the American individualist tradition of democratic governance. Nonetheless, it often works poorly, especially when large numbers of voters know little of consequence about the person. What's more, the person in Congress usually votes with his party these days. The pronounced decline of "party thinking" leaves many voters ill equipped to express effectively the dissatisfaction they clearly feel. Voters don't like important aspects of legislative performance, for example, but voting "for the person" denies them the means of doing much to address their dissatisfaction.

Our argument is not that parties are unneeded as representative institutions—they are needed—or that weakening parties is generally desirable. Instead, it is that much of the contemporary unease with politics and government isn't the result of a diminished party role and that a strengthening of parties as a general principle might well exacerbate the present distress. As for a revival of what we have called "party thinking," those who believe it is needed ultimately have to make the case.

A SUBSTANTIAL PARTY PRESENCE

Nearly four decades ago, political scientist and historian Clinton Rossiter wrote eloquently on the virtues of a "mixed" party system, one that gives a large role to the institutional parties and at the same time to individual voters. The current assumption in political science, though, is that the mixed system is no more because the party presence has declined so markedly. We think this is a vastly excessive response to current trends and an unbalanced reading of them. Some developments have reduced the party presence. The media, for example, play a much larger role in political communication generally, and in the process of candidate choice in particular, than ever before. And this is mostly at the parties' expense.

At the same time, in other areas we have actually moved toward stronger, and in a way more disciplined, political parties. The vehicle of the new "discipline" isn't institutional sanctions—party leaders being able to "punish" recalcitrant members—but rather growing ideological homogeneity within each of the two major parties. When Rossiter wrote *Parties and Politics in America*, the Democratic congressional party was highly irresponsible and undisciplined. It carried within it competing wings, or factions—each resting on a firm local base—that could agree upon little about how the country should be governed except that they wanted the Democratic party to organize the Congress. *Congressional Quarterly* introduced in 1957 the concept of "conservative coalition" votes in Congress, defining them as ones in which a majority of southern Democrats vote with a majority of Republicans against a majority of northern Democrats. "Conservative coalition voting scores" for individual members were a key *Congressional Quarterly* tally. The Democratic party was, then, highly irresponsible, in the sense that its southern wing often worked for aims contrary to what the national party proclaimed. And while the Republicans lacked a split as wide and deep as that between the Democrats' northern and southern wings, liberal, moderate, and conservative blocs detracted from the programmatic coherence of congressional Republicanism as well.

In recent years, however, there has been a powerful movement toward greater "discipline," through the vehicle of internal philosophical agreement. Congressional Democrats are today a much more coherent liberal party, and congressional Republicans a much more conservative one than ever before. We can see this from the splendid roll call analysis done by political scientist William Schneider and his colleagues at *National Journal*. In their January 1991 report, for example, Richard E. Cohen and William Schneider noted that "bipartisanship was a rare commodity on key congressional votes in 1990. And divisions within each party narrowed, according to *National Journal*'s annual congressional vote ratings. . . . Southern Democrats and eastern Republicans, the traditional centers of ideological moderation in both the House and Senate, moved further apart in 1990. Their shifts (the southern Democrats to the left and the eastern Republicans to the right) were another sign of the increased partisanship [i.e., united parties arrayed against each other] in both chambers."

Cohen and Schneider's 1994 report reiterated similar findings and gave powerful evidence of the new-found discipline of both congressional parties.

> Although Congress focused in 1993 on setting new priorities for the national economy, its vigorous partisan divisions ran across the range of issues. On social and foreign policy issues, as well as on economic ones, few Members of either party were inclined toward bipartisan accommodation, a review of last year's major votes reveals. Even regional groupings that typically stood at the political center during the Reagan and Bush presidencies were far apart in 1993 in their ideological rankings. In the House, according to *National Journal's* annual congressional vote ratings, Democrats had an average liberal score of 67 (on a percentile scale of 0–99) and Republicans had an average conservative score of 76 across all three issue areas, with no more than two points separating either party's scores in the three voting categories.

In the 1996 ratings, Cohen and Schneider show that the twenty most liberal senators and the twenty-three most liberal House members were all Democrats, and the twenty most conservative senators and the twenty-two most conservative House members were all Republicans.

A FINAL WORD

Today's mixed system is different from the one Rossiter described, but the party system now contains its own distinctive strengths as well as new elements of weakness. The parties are much more programmatically coherent and internally disciplined by ideological agreement than were those of Rossiter's time. They present far clearer choices for all who care to pay attention. Advocates of stronger and more responsible parties have for the most part failed to call attention to the marked party strengthening evident in the data on the internal coherence of the congressional Republican and Democratic parties.

The United States needs a mixed system—and it has one. Parties have been weakened in some regards but strengthened in others. They remain a substantial presence in American political life; they remain about as much of a presence as the public wants or will abide. And, it is far from clear that the goal of groups such as the Committee for Party Renewal—namely, to have a generalized strengthening of parties, as organizations and in government—would address the principal source of voter complaint, which involves a sense of partisan unresponsiveness and of a politics too dominated by institutions "inside the beltway."

NOTE

The author wants to express his appreciation to Regina Dougherty Rodgers, doctoral student in political science at the University of Connecticut; Cathy Cuneo, his administrative assistant, and Lynn Zayachkiwsky, manager of publications at the Roper Center, for their work in preparing the manuscript; and to Marianne Simonoff, research associate to the director.

5

Intellectual Challenges Facing the Republican Party

JOHN J. PITNEY JR.

In November 1988, astute political observers believed the following: First, because Republicans had won five of the past six presidential elections, the GOP had a "lock" on the Electoral College. Second, because Democrats had controlled the House for thirty-four years, and Republicans had never won more than 192 seats since the 1950s, a GOP majority was a practical impossibility. Third, because House Republicans had long relied on safe, establishmentarian leaders such as Bob Michel, they would never hand a major post to an idea-monger such as Newt Gingrich. Fourth, because the presidential party had lost House seats in every midterm congressional election since 1934, the out-party could always count on the midterm to pad its strength.

Had our 1988 pundits passed through a time warp to 1998, they would have found all of these propositions in tatters. They would have had another surprise, too. Gingrich, who had always been a font of policy proposals and futuristic visions, resigned from Congress and the speakership after many Republicans blamed their leadership for failing to articulate a clear campaign message.

GOP history made this disarray especially puzzling, since the party had often been creative when the Democrats held the White House. After the 1964 Johnson landslide, national GOP leaders worked hard to pose alternatives to the Great Society, and their party made a comeback in the 1966 midterm and 1968 presidential elections.[1] A decade later, in Watergate's wake, Republicans built up their national organization and blazoned new ideas such as supply-side economics.[2]

By the turn of the new century, however, they were looking more like the Democrats of the Nixon and Reagan years, mired in factions and groping for direction.[3]

Why the identity change? As the good-government groups like to say, an out-party needs a positive message that tells how its policies would help the country. But this positive message hinges upon a convincing critique of the in-party's reign; that is, the out-party must diagnose the illness before selling the cure. In the mid-1960s, the GOP could build its agenda on the rubble of Vietnam and the Great Society. In the late 1970s, it could make its case for supply-side economics and "peace through strength" by pointing to Carter's shaky response to stagflation and foreign crises. An out-party's job gets tougher if the in-party can claim a record of peace and prosperity, or if it filches the out-party's policies and themes. That is what happened to the Democrats when Nixon and Reagan sought reelection. In 1972, the economy was growing and the Vietnam War was ending. And to an extent largely forgotten today, Nixon coopted Democratic programs: wage-price regulation, environmental protection, health-care reform, and a guaranteed income.[4] "Tory men and Liberal policies," he said, "are what have changed the world."[5] Reagan flanked the Democrats by quoting their favorite presidents and, more important, by casting himself as the outsider fighting an entrenched Washington establishment.[6] In different ways, Nixon and Reagan thus assumed important elements of the Democrats' own identity. No wonder they were confused.

Unfortunately for the Republicans, Clinton studied the Nixon and Reagan playbooks. Before examining the struggle between Clinton and the GOP, however, we need to step back and examine some major currents of party thought. Republicans ran into trouble not just because of a wily opponent but because of some conflicts and contradictions in their own minds.

CONSERVATISM AND REPUBLICANISM

Humorist Art Buchwald once cracked that the Republican Party has three wings: a right wing, a righter wing, and a rightest wing. There is some truth to that joke. Not since the 1960s has there been a clear affirmative liberal stream of thought in the GOP.[7] Republican elected officials who call themselves "moderates" have inherent difficulties in spelling out a distinctive viewpoint.[8] "Moderation" may be an effective political approach in certain settings, but it is no more an ideology than "pastel" is a color: it is merely a muted version of something else. To find Republican ideas, one must look to the right.

Some distinctions are in order. American intellectual conservatism is not a monolithic movement but a set of quarrelsome factions. Its fault lines pit neoconservatives against paleoconservatives, supply-siders against monetarists, traditionalists against libertarians, Randians against anti-Randians, Straussians against anti-Straussians, and West Coast Straussians against East Coast Straussians.[9] (Even this listing would start a fight. Libertarians often spurn the "conservative" label, while strict Randians consider themselves neither conservative nor libertarian.[10]) These conflicts play out in such publications as *National Review*, *Modern Age*, and *Chronicles*, and in organizations such as the Rockford, Claremont, and Cato institutes.

Republican politicians and staffers see this world as a salad bar of words and ideas. They choose eclectically, here lifting a policy idea from libertarian Milton Friedman, and there borrowing an applause line from traditionalist William Bennett. Seldom does a practical political figure identify strictly with any faction of the intellectual right. For instance, true libertarians—those with a laissez-faire approach to both economics and social issues such as abortion and drug control—are plentiful in think tanks and magazines, but rare among elected officials.[11] In part, this distinction exists because intellectuals and politicians argue about different things. Conservative philosophers debate the true meaning of the Declaration of Independence, whereas GOP politicians seldom mention the document, except at Fourth of July picnics. Conversely, officials have to handle issues on which the intellectual factions may give scant guidance: there is no "Straussian" position on solid waste disposal. The two worlds also have different incentive systems, since intellectuals answer only to small readerships, while politicians must court broad constituencies. Rigorous adherence to the doctrine of limited government is less risky for a *National Review* writer than for a Republican lawmaker facing a roomful of Social Security recipients. "I am a man of principle," explained the late Senator Everett Dirksen (R-IL), "and one of my main principles is flexibility."

A lengthy discussion of conservative taxonomy would cast only a faint light on the GOP. Nevertheless, one may still identify some broad currents of Republican thought. These "currents" consist not of systematic doctrines but of general attitudes toward social change, which one may label roughly as *fundamentalist, orthodox*, and *reform*. Although I borrow the terms from theology, these currents are less about religious beliefs than time perspectives. The *fundamentalist* current (which includes, but is not limited to, religious fundamentalism) looks to the *past*, seeking a return to principles from which America has drifted. The *orthodox* current looks to the *present*, hoping neither for restoration nor revolution, but stability. The *reform* current looks to the *future*, placing its faith in social change, often resulting from the dynamism of free markets.[12]

We now examine each in turn.

FUNDAMENTALIST REPUBLICANISM

It is not a put-down to say that the fundamentalist current would turn back the clock. C. S. Lewis wrote: "Would you think I was joking if I said that you can put a clock back, and if the clock is wrong it is often a very sensible thing to do?" Switching metaphors, he said: "If you are on the wrong road, progress means doing an about-turn and walking back to the right road; and in that case the man who turns back soonest is the most progressive man."[13]

Fundamentalist Republicans believe that their party has strayed from true conservatism, and that the nation has to return to its roots. Alan Keyes, the most dynamic voice for the fundamentalist point of view in the 2000 primary campaign, put it this way: "I think it is vitally important that we understand the real nature of the challenge we face right now. How do we get back to the solid ground of our moral integrity? I think it is quite clear. We must renew our allegiance to the fundamental principle, the simple truth, that we have abandoned: that our rights come from God, and must be exercised with respect for the authority of God."[14] Seeing moral relativism as a central heresy of our time, the fundamentalist Republicans would enact laws banning or curbing abortion, pornography, and gambling. They would support the autonomy of the traditional two-parent family through tax relief and educational choice plans that would allow the use of vouchers at religious schools.[15] Knowing that many voters shy away from sectarian appeals, fundamentalist Republicans prefer to call themselves "pro-family," and one of their major groups is the Family Research Council. In spite of its name, the Christian Coalition has tried to broaden its appeal by saying of its program: "This is not a Christian Agenda. It is not a Republican agenda. It is not a special interest agenda. It is a pro-family agenda, and it is supported by the vast majority of the American people, Republican and Democrat, Christian and Jew, black and white, Protestant and Catholic."[16]

In the sense that we use the term here, political fundamentalism includes more than religious or pro-family issues. This current of thought sees danger in the economy as well as the culture. Pat Buchanan, the clearest representative of the fundamentalist wing in the 1992 and 1996 presidential campaigns, frowned on high technology and immigration, doubting the country's ability to handle the resulting economic changes. As he told the Chicago Council on Foreign Relations in 1998, before his switch to the Reform Party, he wants the GOP to abandon the ideology of free trade, which he called an "alien import, an invention of European academics and scribblers . . . all of whom were repudiated by America's greatest statesmen, including all four presidents on Mount Rushmore." He said that the party should instead turn to "economic nationalism," an attitude that he defined this way: "To me, the country comes before the economy; and the economy exists for the people. I believe in free markets, but I do not worship them. In the proper hierarchy of things, it is the market that must be harnessed to work for man—and not the other way around."[17]

On economic issues, the political fundamentalists share common ground with elements of the political left.[18] Many progressive organizations have attacked the global high-tech economy as a threat to American jobs, and some have also called for curbs on immigration. In his Chicago speech, Buchanan was candid about this odd affinity, quoting Karl Marx's critique of free trade: "Marx was right. Here, then, is the first cost of open-borders free trade. It exacerbates the divisions between capital and labor. It separates societies into contending classes, and deepens the division between rich and poor." Leftist writers have taken note of their new friends. In 1998, Robert Borosage, former director of the Institute for Policy Studies, wrote: "With the contradictions between free markets and strong families, between global corporations and love of country growing increasingly stark, more and more conservatives are questioning the laissez-faire corporate globalism that has enjoyed bipartisan support for two decades."[19]

By combining moralism with distrust of corporate capitalism, the fundamentalists recall the populists of the 1890s. Though one should avoiding stretching the analogy too far—there is no more talk of "free silver"—one can still detect some century-old echoes. Like the populists, the Republican fundamentalists think of themselves as outsiders who stand with the little guys against the special interests. Gary Bauer, a champion of the fundamentalist current in the 2000 nomination campaign, proposed that "we take power out of the hands of Washington and return it, not to huge corporations and Wall Street investment managers, but to America's families." His tax plan called for imposing a flat rate on family income and capital gains alike, and "bringing roughly $800 billion of currently exempt corporate property into the tax base." He condemned big-business Republicans who would invest in things instead of people, and who would "allow our corporate friends to pay zero while secretaries, cab drivers, waitresses, farmers and schoolteachers pay 17 percent."[20]

Republican fundamentalists generally believe that most Americans sympathize with their views, hence the name of the now-defunct "Moral Majority." The real problem, they think, lies with elites in the universities, the major corporations, the mass media, and the Washington power networks. On social issues, do the fundamentalists speak for average voters? Most Americans think abortion should be legal in cases of rape, incest, birth defect, or threat to the mother's health, but not for other circumstances.[21] At the same time, however, a large majority opposes the fundamentalists' favored solution, a constitutional amendment to forbid abortion.[22] William McGurn, formerly Washington bureau chief for *National Review*, put the case clearly: "A constitutional amendment prohibiting all abortions has always been a fiction. Although most Americans are firmly against abortion on demand . . . most do not want abortion completely proscribed. This means that continuing to hold out for a constitutional amendment essentially guarantees that there will be no restrictions at all."[23]

On immigration, fundamentalist views run the risk of backlash. There may be wide skepticism about unlimited immigration, but in most of the country, the opposition lacks intensity.[24] The voters who feel most strongly about immigration are Latino-Americans, the fastest-growing ethnic group in the electorate. Latinos support immigration, and in the pivotal state of California, their support has become an enormous advantage to the Democrats.

ORTHODOX REPUBLICANISM

Orthodox Republicans do not want to turn the clock back—or forward. They are conservative in the situational or Burkean sense, for they support the established social order, whatever it may be at any given time.[25] Of recent GOP presidential nominees, Nixon, Ford, George H. Bush, and Dole all belonged to this current of thought. Although orthodox Republicans often take moderately conservative positions on social issues, they prefer to talk about their support for balanced budgets and reduced regulation. It is hard to describe their "philosophy" because they have a Burkean aversion to abstractions: witness George H. Bush's dismissal of "the vision thing" and Dole's constant refrain of "whatever." Instead of airy promises, they take pride in their ability to get things done. Ironically, they agree with Michael Dukakis that elections are not about ideology but competence.

If the fundamentalists are outsiders, the orthodox Republicans belong to what James Ceaser calls the "insider" tradition of American politics.[26] This tradition, which goes all the way back to the court party of Georgian England and the Federalists of the American Founding, stresses professionalism, pragmatism, and quiet compromise. The insiders would rather strike an agreement than a pose, and they look with suspicion on demagogic appeals to popular opinion. The insider, or orthodox, strain has been dominant for much of American political history, particularly in the Republican Party. One might describe the orthodox current as the GOP's "default option," for without a strong surge from one of the other currents, it is the tendency to which the party naturally reverts. After nominating Goldwater in 1964, the party then turned to Nixon and Ford, and after Reagan came Bush and Dole. When Gingrich quit the House speakership in 1998, his first heir apparent was Bob Livingston of Louisiana, an insider who had chaired the citadel of incrementalism, the Appropriations Committee.

Livingston also quit, after the story of an extramarital affair compromised his support for President Clinton's impeachment. Into his place stepped Denny Hastert of Illinois, a genial conciliator in the mold of Bob Michel, the cautious GOP leader who came before Gingrich.

Orthodox Republicanism promises safety and reliability. As A. James Reichley shrewdly observes, GOP traditionalists make an important contribution to their party when they stress fiscal responsibility and noneconomic values such as social cohesion.[27] They supply the *gravitas* that the fundamentalist and reform strains often lack. But the orthodox have the defect of their virtue, since they offer a slow pace without much sense of direction. Over time, orthodoxy may mean a loss of intellectual vigor and political morale. The Reagan Revolution had dimmed by 1988; and when Bush came in, the lights went out. President Bush had little interest in domestic policy and OMB Director Richard Darman abused aides and officials who espoused ideas other than Darman's. John Podhoretz, a Bush speechwriter, later said: "The end result was at the meeting where the president's top advisers gathered to consider what counsel to give him, aides did not feel free, and were not free, to discuss, dissent from or make recommendations on policy."[28] Gloom spread throughout the reelection campaign and the party as a whole. According to Bush campaign aide Ruth Shalit: "'He who has ideas,' wrote Diderot, 'has style immediately.' The Bush campaign turned out to have no ideas, and so formlessness followed functionlessness."[29]

A similar problem plagued the Dole campaign four years later. At various times, he played to other schools of thought in the party, but was never convincing. He tried to rouse fundamentalists by attacking Hollywood, but the tactic dissolved into tatters when it turned out that he had not seen the movies he was criticizing. He also tried to appeal to economic conservatives by talking about taxes. Normally, that approach would be quite sensible, except that in trying to make a broad pitch, Dole took up contradictory positions. According to his campaign website, Dole wanted "a fairer, flatter, simpler tax system so people can fill out their tax returns without a lawyer, an accountant, or both." But the very same issue release called him "a leading advocate of family tax relief, such as a $500 per child tax credit, 'marriage penalty' relief, adoption tax credits, IRAs for homemakers, and easing the estate tax burden on family businesses."[30] He apparently failed to realize that the second set of proposals would make the tax code more complicated, thereby defeating the goal of tax simplification.

In the early days of the 2000 campaign, the candidate who most clearly represented the orthodox strain was—not surprisingly—Elizabeth Dole. Having spent her entire career as a Washington insider, she made rhetorical bows to conservatism without offering any proposals that would shake the Beltway establishment.

REFORM REPUBLICANISM

Looking at a clock, reformers want to push it ahead—or better yet, reinvent it. During the Progressive Era, "reform Republicans" thought that bureaucratic, centralized, and "scientific" government would cure the corruption and inefficiency of American politics. In the late twentieth century, most reform Republicans believe that such government is not the solution, but the problem. That phrase, of course, comes from President Reagan's 1981 inaugural address. Although Reagan's rhetoric enchanted the fundamentalists, he downplayed their social issues in favor of an economic agenda that drew from the reform current. Reagan's favorite quotation came not from Edmund Burke, but from Burke's foe, Tom Paine: "We have it in our power to begin the world over again." In the words of speechwriter Peggy Noonan, Reagan "was never misty-eyed about the past, he was misty-eyed about the future."[31]

In a 1997 commencement address, Steve Forbes caught the essence of reform Republicanism, a vivid contrast to the Buchanan worldview. The dynamic of this "new age," he said, is "antihierarchical, antiauthoritarian." He criticized those who regard economic transformations as a threat to working people: "This is absolutely not true . . . Whether it is wands or lasers, virtually anyone can get the hang of [business] equipment. The fear that less skilled workers will be left behind in the labor force is unfounded.[32]

In their emphasis on "vision" and "revolution," the reform Republicans differ from the orthodox. They diverge from the conservative fundamentalists by blaming social welfare problems less on moral decline and more on government failure. The 1992 GOP platform, drafted largely by reformists, said: "At a time when the rest of the world has rejected socialism, there are communities here at home where free markets have not been permitted to flourish [and where] people are at the mercy of government. We are determined to elevate the poor into the pro-growth economy."[33]

In a 1990 speech to the World Future Society (a symbolically significant venue), and in subsequent addresses, Bush White House aide James Pinkerton described contemporary reformism as a "New Paradigm" for public policy in the postindustrial age.[34] The New Paradigm, he said, comprises five principles: market forces, individual choice, empowerment, decentralization, and a pragmatic focus on outcomes. Examples of New Paradigm policies would include school choice, tenant ownership of public housing, and enterprise zones.

Reform Republicans have built a promising electoral record. Wisconsin Governor Tommy Thompson used New Paradigm ideas on education and welfare reform to revive the state GOP and win four terms in the state that was the cradle of liberal social policy. Taking a similar approach, Governor John Engler dominated Michigan politics throughout the 1990s. Most dramatically, Bret Schundler campaigned on a message of empowerment to win the mayor's office in overwhelmingly Democratic Jersey City.

Despite these successes, reform Republicans have to grapple with problems, including rocky implementation of their proposals. Tenant management of public housing, a flagship idea of Bush HUD Secretary Jack Kemp and other reformists, has had some high-profile failures involving corruption and crime.[35] And as some libertarian writers have noted, devolution of authority may have the perverse effect of increasing government power, because states and localities often lack the checks and balances that curb abuses at the federal level. Government that is "closer" to the people may actually be more intrusive.[36]

Reform Republicanism has political difficulties, too. Many of its ideas appeal to people who do not yet vote Republican—which is fine for broadening the party's base, but irrelevant to winning primaries. As one may see in Kemp's failed bid for the 1988 presidential nomination, GOP primary voters have little enthusiasm for issues such as tenant management of public housing. Kemp did land the vice presidential nomination in 1996, but there is no evidence that his candidacy did the party any good. With Dole at the top of the ticket, no one could seriously argue that the GOP was running under the banner of innovation and reform. But even if Kemp had been the presidential nominee, the GOP would still have had a hard time claiming this banner, because Bill Clinton had been clutching it for years.

In the 2000 nomination race, the reform current did not appear to have a single, unambiguous standard-bearer. At the start, Forbes appeared likely to capture the flag of reform, but he increasingly stressed social issues and allied himself with fundamentalists such as Paul Weyrich. Senator John McCain enjoyed a vogue as the "reform" candidate because of his advocacy of restrictive campaign-finance legislation. On other issues, however, his positions were either sketchy or incremental.

Texas Governor George W. Bush presented the most ambiguous case: depending on one's point of view, he was either a coalition-builder or a shape-shifter. Obviously, he had family roots in orthodox Republicanism, making him a favorite of party regulars. In the South Carolina primary, he strenuously courted fundamentalists, to the point of making an ill-advised visit to Bob Jones University, an institution that even Pat Robertson regarded as extreme. At other times, his campaign also showed a streak of reformism. Contrary to myth, the younger Bush did not invent the catch phrase "compassionate conservatism;" a decade earlier, it had been a rallying cry for Jack Kemp, Newt Gingrich, and other reformers.[37] As in informal adviser to his father, Bush sympathized with this group, and as a presidential candidate, he actively sought their advice and support. Indianapolis Mayor Stephen Goldsmith, a pioneer of municipal privatization, had a major early role in shaping Bush's policy agenda.[38] After McCain emerged as his major competitor for the nomination, Bush started calling himself "a reformer with results." The new slogan perfectly captured his effort to blend reformation and orthodoxy.

PARADIGMS LOST AND REGAINED

In 1991 and 1992, while senior officials of the elder Bush's administration were ignoring Pinkerton's arguments, certain elements of the Democratic Party were getting the message. Elaine Ciulla Kamarck, a senior fellow of the Progressive Policy Institute (affiliated with the Democratic Leadership Council), wrote that the decades-long debate between laissez-faire and centralized top-down government was now obsolete. She cited the rise of the global information-based economy, the failure of large bureaucracies, the development of new organizational structures, and the absurdity of tax and spending policies that widened the deficit while benefiting the undeserving. "These are the bases of the new politics of the 1990s," she wrote, "and the race is on to see which political party can fashion a philosophy which mirrors the changes that are taking place in the rest of society."[39] According to journalist Mickey Kaus, Arkansas Governor Bill Clinton was bent on winning that race: "The presidential candidate who has discussed Pinkerton's ideas unbidden, obsessively, is Clinton. . . . In mid-1991, as chair of the Democratic Leadership Council, Clinton delivered a speech Pinkerton could easily have written. 'In the Information Age,' Clinton said, Democrats could not rely on 'monopoly decisions handed down from on high by government bureaucracies . . . ' They needed to "reinvent government."[40]

Throughout both the campaign and his presidency, Clinton continued to echo New Paradigm themes. A comparison of statements by Pinkerton and Clinton (below) suggests the extent to which they mined the same intellectual ore. The comparison also points up one of Clinton's fundamental traits: his capacity to adopt policies and phrases that will serve his political purposes.

Market Forces

> PINKERTON: "Governments are now subject to market forces in a way they haven't been before. The official who tinkers with the economy, who pushes the wrong policy button, will see the flow of capital and investment re-route itself instantaneously across nations and continents and oceans."[41]

> CLINTON: "In the emerging global economy, everything is mobile: capital, factories, even entire industries. . . . We believe in free enterprise and the power of market forces."[42]

Choice

> PINKERTON: "The New Paradigm is characterized by increasing individual choice. . . . Up to now, bureaucrats have been

the ones to decide what makes a good public school. President Bush believes that parents should have a say—the final say."

CLINTON: "I'm all for students having more choices. We've worked hard to expand public school choice [including] charter schools that have no rules. They're free of bureaucracy and can only stay in existence if they perform and teach children."[43]

Empowerment

PINKERTON: "The New Paradigm is characterized by policies that empower people to make choices for themselves."

CLINTON: "You know, there's a lot of talk in Washington about empowerment. Sometimes people in the other party mean giving people more choice, but not caring much about whether they can exercise the choice. Well, we want empowerment, too. We want to make sure every person, every family, every community has what it takes to make the most of their own lives and live up to their dreams."[44]

Decentralization

PINKERTON: "The New Paradigm is characterized by decentralization. Authority is dispersing as bureaucracy is devolving. Stalinist governments in Eastern Europe, stodgy corporations on Park Avenue, sclerotic city halls here at home, socialist ministries in the Third World—all are changing."

CLINTON: "People don't want some top-down bureaucracy telling them what to do anymore. That's one reason they tore down the Berlin Wall and threw out communist regimes in Eastern Europe and Russia. Now, the New Covenant will challenge our government to change its way of doing business too."[45]

What works

PINKERTON: "The New Paradigm implies an emphasis on what works. . . . The Old Paradigm stresses input. It measures how

well we do by how much we spend. . . . This defies common
sense, but defiance of common sense is what the Old Paradigm is all about. Bureaucracy elevates Standard Operating
Procedure and regulation above the practical."

CLINTON: "I want every one of you to change the way we
measure the performance of your agencies and the front-line
regulators. . . . I believe safety inspections should be judged,
for example, by how many companies on their watch comply,
not by how many citations our regulators write. We ought to
be interested in results, not process."[46]

What is more, Clinton also lifted the most appealing lines of the
other GOP currents of thought. From orthodox, he took the themes
of "responsibility" and "security." And he coopted two of the fundamentalists' favorite ideas, "faith" and "family." This effort to seize
GOP territory was not mere rhetoric, but a central element of his
approach to public policy. In a memo that became a campaign talis-
man, political advisor Dick Morris described the strategy in explicit
terms: "Fast-forward the Gingrich agenda so that the deficit is reduced, welfare is reformed, the size of government is cut, and regulations are reduced. This will make the Republican issues less appealing
since they will be on their way to solution."[47] Under Clinton, the
federal government indeed made progress toward these goals. Critics
argued that he was the lucky beneficiary of Alan Greenspan's mon-
etary policy and the GOP Congress's legislative accomplishments. Such
criticism may have been valid, but it was also politically irrelevant.
Economic growth, welfare reform, and deficit reduction all happened
during his tenure, so he got the credit. Where did that leave the GOP?

THE REPUBLICAN RIPOSTE

Faced with a Democratic president who took their best lines, Republicans tried to highlight a gap between rhetoric and reality, between
the poetry of his speeches and the prose of his programs. In shooting
at Clinton's image as a New Democrat, Republicans cited the massive
tax increases in the 1993 budget package, as well as the huge cost of

the administration's first-term health-care proposal. As for traditional morality, Republicans raised questions about Clinton policies toward gays in the military and condom distribution in schools. In the early years, some Republican leaders argued that their party should continue to accentuate the negative. Tom DeLay (R-Texas), then secretary of the House Republican Conference, put it this way in 1993: "As long as we're kicking them in the shins and giving them a black eye, we're doing okay."[48] But as of early 1994, evidence started to mount that a purely negative strategy would fail. In a survey on the president's economic plan, only 28 percent of respondents said that Republicans were interested in a realistic alternative, compared with 60 percent who said the GOP was opposing it for political reasons.[49]

Accordingly, the House Republicans developed the Contract with America, a list of ten proposals that they promised to bring to the House floor if they won a majority. Newt Gingrich, the GOP whip who was in line to lead the party, said that the GOP intended their message for "all those who are tired of negative attacks, smear campaigns, for all those who have asked political parties to get together and be a responsible team, for all those who said we have to deal in a positive way with the challenges of America's future . . ."[50] Although most voters did not hear of the Contract per se, it did improve the GOP's fortunes by providing candidates with a ready-made set of positions that they could adapt to their local constituencies.[51]

In the first hundred days of the 105th Congress, the House Republicans kept their word by bringing all the Contract items before the chamber. There is a common misconception that this action backfired by drawing voter attention to the GOP's "extreme agenda." Not so: with House action on the Contract, public approval of Congress increased.[52] And the Contract did leave its mark on the lawbooks. The 104th Congress saw enactment of the Congressional Accountability Act (bringing Congress in compliance with regulations applying to the private sector), the item veto (later ruled unconstitutional by the Supreme Court), and a far-reaching welfare reform bill. In the 105th Congress, the budget agreement included other Contract items: a $500-per-child tax cut, "American Dream" savings accounts, and tax reductions on capital gains. Such successes, however, had a steep political downside for the GOP: every time Clinton signed such a measure, he deprived Republicans of another issue and further blurred party distinctions.

The Contract had other side effects. It created an illusion that the House Republicans enjoyed extraordinary unity and that their leaders had awesome legislative skills. In fact, the House could act so fast only because the Contract consisted of items with a preexisting GOP consensus: the party leadership excluded divisive issues such as abortion. This illusion raised expectations among the attentive public, and it also encouraged hubris within GOP ranks. Republicans paid the price several months later, when they stumbled into a government shutdown that allowed President Clinton to portray them as extremists. By early 1996, they had fallen into a defensive posture from which they never fully recovered.

And inevitably, the congressional agenda moved from the consensus items of the Contract to matters that highlighted differences among the party's currents of thought. The fundamentalists fought the orthodox and reform Republicans over such issues as funding for international groups that promote abortion, and congressional approval of most-favored-nation trade status for China. The reformists won a legislative victory when Congress approved a proposal by Senator Spencer Abraham (R-MI) to increase the number of visas for computer programmers and other skilled workers. Pat Buchanan, however, did not see it as a victory: "This slap in the face of American workers cannot be allowed to stand! The greed of these high-tech corporations, who would rather import foreigners for high-tech jobs than pay Americans the going rate, should not dictate the immigration policy of the United States. It's just that simple."[53] In 1998, an official of the U.S. Chamber of Commerce told *National Journal* that the Republicans "look a lot like the Democratic Party did 15 years ago. If you're in the leadership, you have an awful lot of balancing to do to keep the constituencies happy."[54]

Taxes were another point of contention. Fundamentalists such as Gary Bauer favored "family-friendly" tax cuts that would eliminate the "marriage penalty" and provide greater incentives for childbearing. The reformists wanted to scrap the existing tax code, but split on whether its replacement should be a flat income tax or a national sales tax. As usual, the orthodox worried about moving too fast in any direction. Republican pollster Glen Bolger said: "It's hard to draw distinctions with the Democrats, when internally we don't know, as a party, how to be unified on the issue."[55]

Even if they had found a single message, the tax issue did not have the same power as in years past. Two decades earlier, inflation and static tax brackets had combined to raise individual taxes, thereby kindling support for such measures as the Kemp-Roth tax-cut bill and California's Proposition Thirteen. During this period, the rising generation of GOP politicians—including a freshman from Georgia named Newt Gingrich—drew the lesson that tax cuts were the "crown jewel" of the Republican message. In 1998, as leaders from this generation stood deep in middle age, they had trouble applying the great lesson of their youth. In sharp contrast to the stagflation of the late 1970s, the economy now featured high growth and low inflation. "National malaise" and tax-bracket creep were buried in the closet of American memory, along with gasoline lines and polyester leisure suits. At half past Clinton, there was simply no great call for radical change in the revenue code. And if any embers of tax-cut sentiment were still burning, Clinton crushed them by saying that the budget surplus should go to "saving Social Security first" instead of financing tax cuts. Though Republicans charged that the argument was specious, it was nevertheless politically effective.

In 1998, presidential impeachment had unanticipated consequences. The controversy distracted congressional Republicans from the task of crafting and passing a positive policy agenda. When voters listened to Republicans on television talk shows, they heard about stained dresses instead of new paradigms, and the party took a dive in the polls. Meanwhile, the Clinton White House shrewdly framed the controversy as a partisan witch hunt, pitting the Democrats against the Gingrich-led Republicans. Because congressional Democrats regarded Gingrich with intense hatred and contempt, this approach rallied them around a president they did not actually trust. The unexpected midterm seat loss led Gingrich to resign, depriving the GOP of a major source of intellectual energy. It also left the House GOP seat margin unmanageably thin, putting Speaker Hastert at the mercy of every small group within the party.

THE REPUBLICAN FUTURE

American political parties have never approached the degree of coherence that the "responsible party" school has long wished for. Since the

Founding, the constitutional principles of federalism, bicameralism, and separation of powers have ensured that parties would be as fragmented as the political system itself. In recent years, the system's centrifugal forces have grown stronger as America has moved from an era of *mass* politics to one of *mosaic* politics.[56] A manageable set of peak associations and television networks has given way to a panorama of niche organizations, boutique advocacy groups, specialized publications, "narrowcasting" services, and websites. Because of the proliferation of such organizations, it is no longer accurate to describe GOP policy making as having a hierarchy or even a "stratarchy."[57] Rather, American political parties are turning into "webs" or "nets," where ideas and information flow in a variety of directions. This development has advantages and disadvantages. On the one hand, "outside" groups can help a party shake off an intellectual torpor and think about new ideas: the Democratic Leadership Council played this role in the late 1980s and early 1990s. On the other hand, they can hinder consensus. If a healthy pluralism is not to degenerate into a self-defeating Babel, the party's emerging elements must try to get along with one another.

In 1990, Newt Gingrich grasped the point in words that would foretell much about how he himself would rise—and fall: "[W]e have to recognize that we have to get used to fighting ourselves at times and we have to recognize that we are in the business of conflict management. We are not in the business of conflict resolution. You only resolve conflicts by kicking people out and that means you become a minority. So, if you intend to be a majority, you have to be willing to live with a lot of conflict because that is the nature of a majority."[58]

In 1999, some Republicans were not willing to live with that level of conflict. New Hampshire Senator Bob Smith, a previously obscure supporter of GOP fundamentalism, won attention by announcing a quixotic presidential bid and then bolting the party in disgust. (He rejoined the fold after the unexpected death of a senior colleague opened up a key committee chairmanship.) Similarly, Pat Buchanan headed for the door, complaining that on issues ranging from free trade to foreign aid, "the Republican elite is, with a few exceptions, remarkably close to Clinton-Gore."[59] Smith and Buchanan both held up Ronald Reagan as a model of how to score a victory under a bold ideological banner. They failed to mention that Reagan won the presidency only after he had moderated his position on social security and other issues, and that he always made a point of accommodating other wings of the party.

The purists' frustration did have some basis, however. There was no denying that many Republicans had an unacknowledged case of Clinton envy, marveling at how he could frame the issues in a way that appealed to the voters, united the Democrats, and often left the GOP looking like a collection of naysaying extremists. He had grabbed political turf that they saw as rightfully theirs, and they were increasingly desperate for a way to take it back.

With the election of George W. Bush, Republicans had some cause for hope. Throughout the campaign, he had managed to unite the party's philosophical groups. His formidable running mate, Dick Cheney, had also earned credibility across the Republican spectrum. The orthodox recalled his service as Gerald Ford's chief of staff and George H. W. Bush's Defense Secretary, while the fundamentalists praised his House voting record on social issues, and the reformists cited his role as Bob Michel's liaison to the GOP Young Turks. Perhaps the ticket's most notable accomplishment consisted of offering a market-based proposal on Social Security reform without encountering the voter backlash that many had expected. Nevertheless, the disputed presidential election results, along with the close party balance in Congress, meant that the new Bush-Cheney Administration would not have an easy time turning ideas into policy.

NOTES

Portions of this chapter originally appeared in "Republican Policymaking After Bush," a paper presented at the annual conference of the Western Political Science Association, Albuquerque, New Mexico, March 12, 1994. The author gratefully acknowledges the assistance of Christen Pierce in preparing this manuscript.

    1. John J. Pitney, Jr., "Republican Alternatives to the Great Society," in *Politics, Professionalism and Power: Modern Party Organization and the Legacy of Ray C. Bliss*, ed. John C. Green (Akron, Ohio: Ray C. Bliss Institute, 1994).

    2. Philip A. Klinkner, chap. 7 in *The Losing Parties: Out-Party National Committees, 1956-1993* (New Haven: Yale University Press, 1994).

3. Jon F. Hale, "In Search of a Message: Democrats in the Post-Great Society Era" in *Politics, Professionalism and Power: Modern Party Organization and the Legacy of Ray C. Bliss,* ed. John C. Green (Akron, Ohio: Ray C. Bliss Institute, 1994).

4. Melvin Small, "Disraeli Redux," chap. 7 in *The Presidency of Richard Nixon* (Lawrence, Kansas: University Press of Kansas, 1999).

5. Quoted in Daniel Patrick Moynihan, *The Politics of a Guaranteed Income: The Administration and the Family Assistance Plan* (New York: Random House, Vintage Books, 1973), 215.

6. Stephen Skowronek, *The Politics Presidents Make: Leadership from John Adams to George Bush* (Cambridge, Massachusetts: Harvard University Press/Belknap, 1993), 414-415.

7. Nicol C. Rae, *The Decline and Fall of the Liberal Republicans from 1952 to the Present* (New York: Oxford University Press, 1989).

8. For a little-noticed attempt to develop a moderate Republican worldview, see: James Leach and William P. McKenzie, eds., *A Newer World: The Progressive Republican Vision of America* (Lanham, Maryland: Madison Books, 1989).

9. The standard work on the subject is: George H. Nash, *The Conservative Intellectual Movement in America since 1945* (New York: Basic Books, 1976). For a sample of conflicting perspectives, see: Paul Gottfried and Thomas Fleming, *The Conservative Movement* (Boston: Twayne, 1988); David Boaz, *Libertarianism: A Primer* (New York: Free Press, 1997); Charles R. Kesler, "All American?" *National Review*, 7 December 1998, 52–55.

10. Friedrich Hayek wrote a famous essay titled "Why I am Not a Conservative" as the postscript to *The Constitution of Liberty* (South Bend: Gateway, 1972 [1960]), 397–411. Ayn Rand resented "being lumped with anyone" (including libertarians) and specifically denounced the conservative *National Review* as "the worst and most dangerous magazine in America." Quoted in Alvin Toffler, "The *Playboy* Interview with Ayn Rand," in *The Libertarian Reader*, ed. David Boaz (New York: Free Press, 1997), 165.

11. For a thoughtful discussion of the relationship between ideology and practical politics, see chapter 3 in Douglas L. Koopman, *Hostile Takeover: The House Republican Party 1980-1995* (Lanham, Maryland: Rowman and Littlefield, 1996).

12. The discussion on this point owes much to chapter 1 in Virginia Postrel, *The Future and Its Enemies: The Growing Conflict Over Creativity, Enterprise, and Progress* (New York: Free Press, 1998).

13. C. S. Lewis, *Mere Christianity* (New York: Macmillan, Collier Books, 1952), 36.

14. Alan Keyes, remarks at Virginia high school, 28 February 2000, at <http://www.keyes2000.org/issues_and_speeches/transcripts/va_hs.shtml> 18 (April 2000).

15. The Family Research Council, a fundamentalist group associated with Dr. James Dobson's Focus on the Family, has detailed many such positions on its website: <http://www.frc.org/faq>.

16. Ralph Reed, "Introduction," in Christian Coalition, *Contract With the American Family* (Nashville: Moorings, 1995), xi.

17. Patrick J. Buchanan, "Free Trade is Not Free," address to the Chicago Council on Foreign Relations, 18 November 1998, at <http://www.theamericancause.org/pjb-speech-chicago-cfr.html> 28 (September1999).

18. Postrel, *The Future and Its Enemies*, 1–4.

19. Robert L. Borosage, "Look Who's Battling Global Capitalists," *Houston Chronicle*, 5 July 1998, Outlook, 1.

20. Gary Bauer, flat tax proposal, at <http://www.bauer2k.com/html/taxplan.html> 27 (September 1999).

21. See the poll data in Harold W. Stanley and Richard G. Niemi, *Vital Statistics on American Politics 1997–1998* (Washington: Congressional Quarterly Press, 1998), 150.

22. Ibid., 143–145.

23. William McGurn, "Abortion and the GOP," *National Review*, 15 March 1993, 52.

24. James G. Gimpel and James R. Edwards, Jr., *The Congressional Politics of Immigration Reform* (Needham Heights, Massachusetts: Allyn and Bacon, 1999), 45.

25. Samuel P. Huntington, "Conservatism as an Ideology," *American Political Science Review* 51 (June 1957): 454–473.

26. James Ceaser and Andrew Busch, *Upside Down and Inside Out: The 1992 Elections and American Politics* (Lanham, Maryland: Rowman and Littlefield/Littlefield Adams Quality Paperbacks, 1993), 2.

27. A. James Reichley, "Republican Ideology and the American Future," in *The Politics of Ideas: Intellectual Challenges to the Major Parties After 1992*, eds. John K. White and John C. Green (Lanham, Maryland: Rowman and Littlefield, 1995), 82–83.

28. John Podhoretz, *Hell of a Ride: Backstage at the White House Follies* (New York: Simon and Schuster, 1993), 63.

29. Ruth Shalit, "What I Saw at the Devolution," *Reason* (March 1993): 27.

30. Quoted in John J. Pitney, Jr., "Tangled Web," *Reason* (April 1996): 52.

31. Quoted in James P. Pinkerton, "Reagan's Legacy—Unbridled Capitalism," *Newsday*, 1 February 1996, A43.

32. Steve Forbes, commencement address at Claremont McKenna College, Claremont, California, 18 May 1997 (privately printed).

33. Republican National Convention, *The Vision Shared: Uniting Our Family, Our Country, and the World* (Houston, Texas: Republican National Convention, 1992), 31.

34. For the most complete descriptions of the idea, see the following works by James P. Pinkerton: "The New Paradigm," remarks to the Reason Foundation, Los Angeles, California, 23 April 1990, and *What Comes Next: The End of Big Government and the New Paradigm Ahead* (New York: Hyperion, 1995).

35. In the fall of 1998, the city of Boston seized management of a 1,200-unit complex as federal agents arrested 28 tenants and indicted 10 others on drug charges. See Associated Press story at: <www.daily.ou.edu/ideas/1998/november-03/boston.html>.

36. Clinton Bolick, *Grassroots Tyranny: The Limits of Federalism* (Washington: Cato Institute, 1993).

37. Douglas Harbrecht, "Look Who's Setting the House on Fire," *Business Week*, 14 August 1989, 94.

38. James A. Barnes, "Inside Bush's Campaign Shop," *National Journal*, 7 August 1999, 2306–2307.

39. Elaine Ciulla Kamarck, "Towards a New Paradigm," *The Mainstream Democrat*, September 1990, 22.

40. Mickey Kaus, "Paradigm's Loss," *The New Republic*, 27 July 1992, 18.

41. All Pinkerton quotations in the table are from his Reason Foundation speech on "The New Paradigm, supra.

42. Bill Clinton and Al Gore, *Putting People First* (New York: Times Books, 1992), 6.

43. Transcript of presidential debate between President Clinton and [former Senator Dole, Hartford, Connecticut, 6 October 1996, at <http://www.pub.whitehouse.gov> (3 December 1998).

44. Bill Clinton, remarks to the Service Employees International Union, Washington, DC, 24 April 1996, at <http://www.pub.whitehouse.gov> (3 December 1998).

45. Bill Clinton, "The New Covenant: Responsibility and Rebuilding the American Community," address at Georgetown University, Washington, DC, 23 October 1991, in Robert E. Levin, *Bill Clinton: The Inside Story* (New York: S.P.I./Shapolsky, 1992), 293.

46. Bill Clinton, remarks at regulatory reform event, Washington, DC, 21 February 1995, at <http://www.pub.whitehouse.gov> 3 (December 1998).

47. Dick Morris, *Behind the Oval Office: Winning the Presidency in the Nineties* (New York: Random House, 1997), 37.

48. Quoted in Kenneth J. Cooper and Kevin Merida, "Republican Dilemma: To Defend the Past or Define the Future," *Washington Post*, 28 February 1993, A4.

49. Charles E. Cook, "GOP Can't Count on Clinton's Woes to Bring '94 Success," *Roll Call*, 10 May 1993, 9.

50. Newt Gingrich, remarks at "Contract with America" event, Washington, DC, 27 September 1994 (Federal News Service transcript).

51. Robin Kolodny, "The Contract with America in the 104th Congress," in *The State of the Parties*, 2d ed., eds. John C. Green and Daniel M. Shea (Lanham, Maryland: Rowman and Littlefield, 1996), 319.

52. In the previous four years, public approval of Congress seldom topped 30 percent. Right after the House finished its initial action on the Contract, the approval rating was 37 percent—not stellar, but an improvement. See the Gallup data at: <http://www.gallup.com/gallup poll data/ratecong/jobapp.htm> (3 December 1998).

53. Open letter by Pat Buchanan, fall 1998, <http://www.theamerican cause.org/issue-h1b-01.html> (3 December 1998).

54. R. Bruce Josten, executive vice president for government affairs at the U.S. Chamber of Commerce, quoted in Peter H. Stone, "Family Feud," *National Journal* 2 May 1998, 987.

55. Quoted in Richard E. Cohen and James A. Barnes, "The Parties Adrift," *National Journal*, 25 April 1998, 918.

56. Alvin Toffler, *PowerShift* (New York: Bantam, 1990), 252-254.

57. A "stratarchy" is a series of organizational layers that are not necessarily dependent on one another. Samuel J. Eldersveld, *Political Parties in American Society* (New York: Basic, 1982), 133.

58. Quoted in William F. Connelly, Jr. and John J. Pitney, Jr., *Congress' Permanent Minority? Republicans in the US House* (Lanham, Maryland: Rowman and Littlefield, 1994), 165.

59. Patrick J. Buchanan, "Malaise of the GOP—Is There a Cure?" 2 February 1999, at <http://www.gopatgo.org/pa-99-0202-gopcure.html> (28 September 1999).

6

Democratic Party Ideology in the 1990s: New Democrats or Modern Republicans?

PHILIP KLINKNER

W ithout a doubt, the most important ideological develop ment in the Democratic Party in the 1990s is the rise of the so-called "New Democrats." First coined by Bill Clinton during his 1992 presidential campaign, the New Democrats sought to craft a series of political and policy stances that would establish a "third way" between what they saw as the outmoded and unpopular tenets of traditional Democratic Party liberalism, and the excessive conservatism of the post-Reagan Republican Party. To its adherents, the development of the New Democrat philosophy has been a stunning success, shifting the Democratic Party to the political center. And, by running as a New Democrat, Bill Clinton not only recaptured the White House for the Democrats, but also became the first Democrat to win a second term since FDR. Furthermore, the New Democrats argue that they have developed a set of policy stands that has effectively stymied the programmatic agenda of the Republican Party and, in the words of Bill Clinton, helped the Democrats "build a bridge to the 21st Century."

Although not without some truth, these claims are highly debatable. Indeed, in this chapter, I will argue that both the political and policy successes of the New Democrats are greatly overstated. Furthermore, the New Democrats have failed to develop both an effective political philosophy and a base of grassroots support, the two factors necessary for them to truly transform American politics. Consequently, the New Democrats are similar to the "Modern Republicans" of the 1950s, a briefly successful party faction that failed in its efforts to reshape the American political landscape.

THE ORIGINS OF THE NEW DEMOCRATS

Although the Democratic Party has experienced tension and conflict between its liberal and conservative wings since its founding over 200 years ago, the direct origins of the New Democrats date back to the intraparty disputes following Walter Mondale's landslide loss to Ronald Reagan in 1984. Many conservative southern Democrats had become increasingly dismayed by the Democrats' electoral prospects. According to Senator Lawton Chiles of Florida, "Most of us had been running away from the Democratic Party for years. But we were beginning to see you couldn't enjoy the luxury of that anymore. Maybe some of us would survive, but there wasn't going to be a Democratic Party behind us in our state."[1] The problem, for many moderate to conservative Democrats, was the perception that the party possessed an outdated ideology and was held captive by various internal "special interests." As one southern party leader put it, "The problem is the public's perception of the Democrats. The perception is that we are the party that can't say no, that caters to special interests and that does not have the interests of the middle class at heart."[2] Others, like former LBJ aide Harry McPherson, were more blunt, "Blacks own the Democratic Party. . . . White Protestant male Democrats are an endangered species."[3]

Frustrated with a Democratic National Committee that they thought was tilted toward liberals and organized labor, party conservatives, mostly from the South and the West, established the Democratic Leadership Council (DLC) in 1985. In its first years, the DLC focused its efforts on creating a southern regional primary that would give that region (and presumably conservative Democrats) more of a voice in the party's nominating process. Though they succeeded in establishing a southern regional primary, dubbed "Super Tuesday," the effort ultimately backfired on the DLC. The big winners on Super Tuesday in 1988 were Jesse Jackson and Michael Dukakis, hardly the sorts of candidates that the DLC hoped to see get the party's nomination.[4]

Following Dukakis's defeat in 1988, the DLC returned to the drawing board to find a new way to shift the Democratic Party to the right. Instead of procedural devices like Super Tuesday, the DLC, according to political scientist Jon Hale, now sought to become "more of an ideas-based movement focused on shaping a specific mainstream alternative identity for the party."[5] As the first step in this process, the DLC published a biting critique of traditional Democratic Party liberalism, *The Politics of Evasion*. Written by political scientists Elaine Kamarck and William Galston, the document declared that the Democrats were held captive to a "liberal fundamentalism" that had "lost touch with the American people." "Since the late 1960s, the public has come to associate liberalism with tax and spend policies that contradict the interests of average families; with welfare policies that foster dependence rather than self-reliance; with softness toward the perpetrators of crime and indifference toward its victims; with ambivalence toward the assertion of American values and interests abroad; and with an adversarial stance toward mainstream moral and cultural values."[6]

Despite their claims to represent the voice of average Americans, the DLC largely failed in its efforts to develop a grassroots organization and the group relied heavily on contributions from corporate and special-interest contributors. As Hale writes, "The annual budget of the post- 1988 institutionalized DLC reached and surpassed the $2 million mark, with corporate sponsorships bringing in substantial portions. Of one hundred DLC Sustaining Members in 1991-1992, fifty-seven were corporations and another twelve were professional or trade associations. The energy, health care, insurance, pharmaceutical, retail, and tobacco industries were all represented."[7]

Although the DLC failed to develop a grassroots organization, it did succeed in raising its public profile, in particular through holding its first convention in Cleveland in 1991. Much of the success of the DLC in these years was due to the efforts of its 1990-1991 chairman, Governor Bill Clinton of Arkansas. Clinton proved an able and popular spokesperson for the DLC and he worked tirelessly to help build the organization.

THE NEW DEMOCRATS AND THE 1992 ELECTION

This relationship paid off for both Clinton and the DLC in 1992. For Clinton, his work with the DLC gave him important connections to the DLC's contributors and activists.[8] For the DLC, Clinton's candidacy provided the vehicle for its policy agenda. Ironically, however, Clinton's success in capturing the Democratic nomination was helped greatly by his ability to outflank his major opponents, Paul Tsongas and Jerry Brown, from the left. During the primaries, Clinton often ran as the economic populist, attacking Tsongas for his preoccupation with deficit reduction and complaining that his economic plan threatened Social Security, and Brown for supporting a regressive "flat" income tax.

With the nomination won, however, Clinton strove in the general election to run as a New Democrat. As Jon Hale points out, the 1992 Democratic platform was remarkably similar to the themes sounded by the DLC: "The text of the platform was organized around the main themes of the New Democrats. Opportunity, Responsibility, Community, and National Security were main headings with specific agenda item subheadings listed underneath these main headings. A comparison of the platform with the DLC's New Choice Platform revealed striking similarities between the two. Of fifty-one specific agenda item subheadings in the platform, thirty-seven were in agreement with agenda items in the DLC's New Choice Draft, and nothing in the platform was in disagreement. None of the positions taken in the fourteen platform items not covered in the New Choice Draft were found to be not in accordance with the gist of the DLC document."[9]

In his acceptance speech, Clinton also spoke to many New Democrat themes. The title of the speech, "The New Covenant," reflected one of the central ideas of the New Democrats—that government efforts to provide greater resources and opportunities must be tied to the expectation of greater personal responsibility. As Clinton said:

> I call this approach a New Covenant—a solemn agreement between people and their government, based not simply on what each of us can take but on what all of us must give to our nation.

> We offer our people a new choice based on old values. We offer opportunity. We demand responsibility. We will build an American community again. The choice we offer is not conservative or liberal. In many ways it's not even Republican or Democratic. It's different. It's new. And it will work.[10]

Though he embraced the New Democrat label in 1992, it is not clear that doing so was instrumental to Clinton's victory. Though he won overwhelmingly in the electoral college, Clinton managed only a relatively narrow five-percentage-point victory over George Bush in the popular vote. In fact, Clinton's percentage was below the 46 percent gained by Michael Dukakis in 1988. Even among white voters—the clear target of the New Democrats' message—Clinton ran behind Dukakis's showing, 39 to 40 percent.[11]

Nonetheless, many argue that Clinton's identification as a New Democrat allowed him to shore up support among crucial constituencies—white males, suburbanites, and moderate southerners—who would otherwise have defected to Bush or Ross Perot if the Democrats had nominated a more liberal candidate. Perhaps, but this analysis overlooks the economic context of the 1992 election. Study after study has shown that indicators of economic performance are the most important influences on presidential election outcomes.[12] In 1992, Bill Clinton had the advantage of running against an incumbent who presided over a sharp economic downturn. Specifically, in 1991, the gross domestic product (GDP) of the U.S. economy fell by 1.2 percent and in 1992 it rose by an anemic 2.1 percent. In 1992, unemployment was 7.5 percent. In contrast, four years earlier, Michael Dukakis ran against a tide of economic prosperity. In 1987 and 1988, however, GDP rose by 3.1 and 3.9 percent respectively, while unemployment in the latter year was only 5.5 percent.[13] All things being equal, there is little reason to doubt that almost any qualified Democrat candidate in 1992 should have improved upon the party's 1988 performance. Indeed, this was the factor behind the Clinton campaign's unofficial slogan of "It's the economy, stupid."

In addition to the advantage of running against an incumbent in a weak economy, Bill Clinton also benefited from the three-way nature of the 1992 presidential election. That year saw the entry, exit, and then reentry of Ross Perot into the campaign. Without a doubt, these events worked to Clinton's benefit. Throughout the campaign, Perot directed most of his attacks at George Bush. In fact, when Perot left the campaign in July, he helped Clinton immensely by citing the "revitalized" Democrats. Perot also helped Clinton by deterring the Bush campaign from launching the types of social and cultural "wedge-issue" attacks that they had used so effectively against Dukakis in

1988. With Perot in the race, such negative attacks might have only succeeded in driving down support for both Clinton and Bush, to the benefit of Perot.

CLINTON, THE NEW DEMOCRATS, AND THE 1994 DEBACLE

Though he entered office with high hopes, the first two years of the Clinton presidency now seem but prologue to the Democratic debacle of 1994. To New Democrats, these two years are a tale of lost opportunity. In their telling, Clinton made a series of crucial missteps. The first of these was his decision, soon after entering office, to allow gays and lesbians to serve in the military. The decision set off a firestorm of opposition and established the perception that once in office, Clinton was really an "old" Democrat, more interested in satisfying marginal and unpopular Democratic Party interest groups at the expense of the broader national interest. Next, the President jettisoned his campaign promise of a middle-class tax cut and developed a deficit-reduction package that was at once too limited and too heavily weighted toward tax increases rather than spending cuts. Next, Clinton chose to move forward on health-care legislation before welfare, thereby losing the chance to cement his New Democrat credentials by reforming the program that had done so much to sour public perceptions of government programs. Finally, the health-care reform package offered by Clinton relied too heavily on government controls and raised the unpopular specter of, as its Republican opponents put it, making medical care as efficient as the Post Office and as compassionate as the IRS. Out of such mistakes, the New Democrats argue, the Republicans took control of Congress in 1994.[14]

The New Democrats are surely right that Clinton made several mistakes in his first two years in office, but it is not clear that Clinton's inability or unwillingness to shed the "Old Democrat" label was the only factor behind the Republicans' success in 1994. Indeed, a strong case can be made that the best explanations for the 1994 election rest elsewhere. First, as in 1992, economic factors appear to have greatly influenced the outcome of the election, thereby weakening the case that the outcome of the campaign rested upon a particular strategy or political label. Though the unemployment rate had fallen from 7.5 to

6.1 percent since 1992, real wages and compensation of workers also fell 2.3 percent from March 1994 to March 1995.[15] Public perceptions of the economy had also failed to improve. Fifty-nine percent of those polled in October 1994 believed that the economy was still in a recession.[16] Exit polls in 1994 showed that only 21 percent of voters thought that their standard of living was getting better, while 55 percent though it was unchanged, and 23 percent thought it was worse.[17]

These economic factors clearly mattered at the polls. As Ruy Teixeira and Joel Rogers have shown, those voters who voted Democratic for Congress in 1992 but then defected to the Republicans in 1994 were heavily concentrated among those who had seen the greatest declines in their economic fortunes. According to Teixeira and Rogers, the "9-point anti-Democratic shift among conservatives (37 percent of the electorate) pales compared to the 25-point shift against the Democrats among those who thought the economy was not so good or poor (about 60 percent of the electorate) and the 36-point Democratic shift among those who thought their family financial situation was getting worse (about a quarter of the electorate)." Thus, much as George Bush had in 1992, Bill Clinton paid the price for a bad economy in 1994.[18]

Second, a portion of the Democrats' losses can be attributed to turnout declines among key Democratic constituencies—minorities and the poor. According to Census data, between 1990 and 1994, voter turnout among those making $50,000 a year or more rose from 59.2 percent to 60.1 percent, but turnout among those making under $5,000 fell from 32.2 percent to 19.9 percent, and from 30.9 percent to 23.3 percent for those making between $5,000 and $10,000. In addition, while white turnout rose slightly, from 46.7 percent in 1990 to 46.9 percent in 1994, black turnout fell from 39.2 percent to 37 percent and Hispanic turnout fell from 23.1 percent to 19.1 percent.[19] It hardly seems reasonable that a stronger identification with New Democrat themes would have helped to boost turnout among these groups.

Finally, Democratic losses in 1994 were also heavily concentrated among Perot voters. In 1992, 54 percent of these voters supported Democratic congressional candidates. Two years later, however, they supported the Republicans by a two-to-one margin, 67 to 33 percent.[20] The movement of these Perot voters was so decisive that only white, born-again Christians, self-identified Republicans, and self-identified conservatives supported Republican candidates more strongly.[21] This shift is also evident in the fact that the average 1992 Perot vote in seats that switched from the Democrats to the Republicans in 1994 was 20.5 percent; in seats that remained Democratic, however, the average Perot vote was only 16 percent. As with lower-income groups and minorities, it seems unlikely that the behavior of these voters was strongly influenced by any perception that Clinton was insufficiently identified as a New Democrat. Perot voters most strongly identified with issues of political corruption and economic nationalism. Of the former, Clinton and the New Democrats had little or nothing to say, and of the latter, both Clinton and the New Democrats were closely identified with free trade and the NAFTA treaty, in contrast with Ross Perot and the bulk of his supporters.[22]

THE 1996 REVIVAL

Stunned by the Democrats' loss of Congress, Bill Clinton sought once again to reposition himself as a New Democrat. Aided by political consultant Dick Morris, Clinton adopted a strategy of triangulation—attempting to position himself as the moderate center between the extremes of traditional Democratic liberalism and the conservatism of Newt Gingrich and the Republican "revolutionaries" of the 104th Congress.[23] Specifically for Clinton, this meant accepting the Republican demand for a balanced budget, though over a longer period of time and in a manner that protected such traditionally Democratic programs as Medicare and education.

Clinton's ability to triangulate was greatly aided by the extremism and intransigence of the congressional Republicans. Particularly after the Oklahoma City bombing, Republican rhetoric about "revolution" and "tearing down the welfare state" seemed at best overstated and perhaps even inflammatory.[24] That fall, congressional Republicans made good on their threat to shut down the federal government and perhaps even default on the federal debt unless President Clinton agreed to their budget proposals. The public, however, consistently blamed Congress for the impasse and the Republicans were forced to make concessions to the President in the ultimate budget agreement. The budget showdown greatly enhanced the President's popularity; by late 1995, he was leading Bob Dole and throughout the 1996 campaign he would never again fall behind.[25]

Though Clinton and the New Democrats would claim that Clinton's moves toward the middle were the key to his success in 1996, as with their explanations of the 1992 and 1994 elections, the real answer appears to lie elsewhere. First and foremost, the economic tide that had run in Clinton's favor in 1992 and then against him in 1994 was once again running to his advantage. With unemployment and prices falling and incomes and the stock market rising, in 1996 Bill Clinton was blessed with one of the best economies in nearly thirty years. Unemployment had fallen to under 5 percent by the time of the election, the lowest rate since the early 1970s.[26]

In addition to the economic tailwind at his back, Bill Clinton also had the advantage of the support of various constituencies that had abandoned him and congressional Democrats in 1994. But in most cases these votes were not motivated by the "values issues" appeals of the New Democrats. In fact, as Ruy Teixeira points out, these voters supported Clinton largely because of his support for such "Old Democrat" issues as Social Security, Medicare, education, and the environment.[27]

Finally, despite Bill Clinton's victory, the Democrats were unable to regain control of Congress. In fact, Clinton had the shortest coattails of any reelected President since Dwight Eisenhower, winning only eight seats in the House and losing two in the Senate (See Table 6-1.)

Table 6–1. Presidential Reelection Coattails

President	Election	House Seat Gain/Loss	Senate Seat Gain/Loss
Eisenhower	1956	−2	0
Johnson	1964	+38	+2
Nixon	1972	+12	−2
Reagan	1984	+14	−2
Clinton	1996	+8	−2

THE PROGRAMMATIC IMPACT OF THE NEW DEMOCRATS

Given that the electoral success of the New Democrats is at best arguable, what then has been their programmatic impact? According to the New Democrats, they have established a series of innovative and effective policies. In particular, they point to the following policy achievements of the Clinton years: family and medical leave, the budget package of 1993, the 1994 crime bill, AmeriCorps, NAFTA and GATT, welfare reform, and the balanced budget.[28] Let us examine these in order:

1. Family and Medical Leave: Though supported by most New Democrats, this bill originated among liberal congressional Democrats in the mid-1980s, long before the New Democrats arrived on the scene.[29]

2. The budget package of 1993—passed by one-vote margins in both the House and the Senate. This budget package is credited by the Clinton administration with helping to point the budget back towards a surplus and with launching the economic recovery of the Clinton years. Even if this were true, it is not at all clear this is a policy achievement for the New Democrats. Though they often cited the need for fiscal responsibility, deficit reduction was not a primary issue of the New Democrats prior to and during the 1992 campaign. Real credit for raising that issue should rightly go to Ross Perot. Furthermore, the particulars of the budget package bear no unique New Democrat stamp. As David Mayhew points out, the 1993 budget agreement bears a remarkable similarity to that put together by Republican President George Bush and the congressional Democrats in 1990. Both were of roughly equal size and both relied on a relatively equal combination of tax increases and spending cuts to achieve their savings. All of this suggests that the 1993 budget was the product of a general consensus on deficit reduction that developed across party lines in the early 1990s.[30]

3. The 1994 crime bill passed in the last days of the 103rd Congress. The bill contained a mix of provisions intended to satisfy both liberals and conservatives. For the former, the bill contained stricter limits on handgun purchases (the Brady bill) and increased spending for anti-crime social programs like drug treatment and midnight basketball. For the latter, there were tougher death penalty provisions. The bill did contain one element that could rightly be linked to the

New Democrats—funding for 100,000 more police on the streets. Even so, the impact of this provision, or indeed of the whole bill itself, on the drop in crime statistics in recent years seems marginal at best. A more plausible explanation is provided by changes in demographic cohorts and a stabilization of the drug trade in many large cities. The most that can be said about the New Democrat aspects of the bill is that they encouraged a general trend toward community policing that has played a supporting role in the drop in crime.

4. Perhaps more than any other piece of legislation in the Clinton years, the creation of AmeriCorps is the clearest reflection of New Democrat ideas. By providing college scholarships to young people engaged in community service activities, the program embodies the New Democrat emphasis on linking opportunity and responsibility. At the same time, AmeriCorps also hearkens back to some earlier, Old Democrat programs— the GI Bill of the Roosevelt administration, the Peace Corps of Kennedy's New Frontier, and the VISTA program of the Great Society. Finally, even if it were the singular responsibility of the New Democrats, AmeriCorps is a tiny program. The program's budget is less than $500 million and only 100,000 people have served in it since its inception in 1994. Any program operating on such a small scale is hardly likely to alter the political landscape.[31]

5. Free trade has always been a central aspect of the New Democrat program. The New Democrats have long stressed that the development of the global economy provides numerous economic opportunities and requires a revamping of traditional Democratic economic policies that stressed support for unions and regulation of industry. Perhaps this is so, but in supporting free trade agreements like NAFTA and GATT, the New Democrats appear to belie their own political logic. The New Democrats have consistently stated the need for the Democrats to rely on pragmatic politics rather than ideological dogma and to represent the national interest as opposed to various special interests. True political pragmatism would suggest at least a softening of the New Democrat stand on free trade since those groups that have been most likely to abandon the Democrats since 1992 are downscale voters, the very people most damaged by free trade and consequent downward pressure on U.S. wages.[32]

6. Welfare reform is often cited as the singular public policy achievement of the New Democrats. When he first ran for president in 1992,

Bill Clinton consistently cited his desire to "end welfare as we know it" as proof that he was indeed a New Democrat. A campaign ad described Clinton and Gore as "a new generation of Democrats. . . . They don't think the way the old Democratic Party did. They've called for an end to welfare as we know it."[33] Though the final version of welfare reform that passed in 1996 bore the clear imprint of congressional Republicans, many of its central features originated with or were supported by President Clinton and other New Democrats. As Clinton promised, this legislation did in fact end welfare as we knew it, eliminating a sixty-year-old program, first enacted during the New Deal, that guaranteed federal support for impoverished families. In its place, the legislation turned responsibility for providing for the poor to the states and established mandatory time limits on the receipt of benefits.

Since its passage, supporters of the legislation have pointed to a sharp drop in welfare caseloads. Such declines have indeed been impressive in some areas, but the number of people on welfare had been declining even before the passage of the law. Additionally, this drop in welfare cases comes during what is perhaps the best job market in nearly thirty years. The true test of a safety net comes when people are falling. Therefore, the verdict remains out on the new legislation until the next economic downturn. Even with a booming economy, recent reports by several private charities noted a sharp upturn in those seeking assistance from food kitchens and homeless shelters. Furthermore, the new law's two-year time limit for assistance has yet to expire for most recipients, leaving open the question of what will happen to those who are unable to find work once their support is cut off.[34]

The central place of welfare reform in the achievements of the New Democrats also points to another issue. In their calls for more "personal responsibility," the New Democrats have tapped into the latent racism of many white Americans. Citing the need for "personal responsibility" was often seen as a shorthand way of absolving the majority of Americans of responsibility for continuing racism and the decline of inner cities. It is surely true that calls for "personal responsibility" can apply to all Americans, but the fact that the most significant implementation of this rhetoric was reform of welfare, the policy area most laden with racial and gender stereotypes, suggests a less than equal application of principle.[35]

7. After seeming to spiral out of control since the early 1980s, the federal budget came into balance in 1998 for the first time in nearly thirty years. To New Democrats, this event is proof that fiscal responsibility and progressive policies need not contradict one another. The balanced budget may be a sign of fiscal responsibility, but it is not a sign of progressive politics. In fact, most of the burden for balancing the budget fell on the backs of the poor, hardly the sort of "shared sacrifice" called for by the New Democrats.[36]

ALTERNATIVES TO THE NEW DEMOCRATS

Despite having dominated the party during the Clinton years, the New Democrats are not the only faction of the Democratic Party. To the right of the New Democrats stand even more conservative Democrats. Largely based in the South, these ranks also include some who would consider themselves "true" New Democrats and take Clinton to task for remaining so wedded to traditional liberal ideals. Although once an important party faction, particularly in the halls of Congress, these conservative Democrats have greatly diminished in both number and influence as the party has shifted to the left and as Republicans have come to dominate national politics in the South. Among the most prominent members of this group are Texas Representative Charles Stenholm and Connecticut Senator Joe Lieberman, Al Gore's 2000 running mate.

To the left of the New Democrats stand two overlapping factions of liberal Democrats. The first of these factions is the traditional New Deal liberals. Often closely aligned with organized labor blue-collar constituencies, these Democrats emphasize bread-and-butter economic issues. Among the leaders of this faction are Iowa Senator Tom Harkin and Michigan Representative David Bonior. The second of the liberal factions is the New Politics Democrats. Although they often share the economic ideas of the New Deal liberals, these liberals place a much greater emphasis on representing the political aspirations of racial and ethnic minorities, women, gays, and lesbians. New Politics Democrats are also more identified with various social issues, such as abortion, the environment, and gun control. Leaders of the New Politics Democrats include Jesse Jackson and Minnesota Senator Paul Wellstone.

The strength of these latter two factions is an open question. On the one hand, such groups are not nearly as strong within the party as they once were. Evidence of this weakness can be seen in former Senator Bill Bradley's unsuccessful effort to wrest the Democratic nomination from Al Gore by attacking him from the left. On the other hand, the 2000 primary campaign might not be the best test of strength for the leftist factions of the Democratic Party, given the great difficulty in taking the nomination away from a sitting Vice President. A judgment on the true center of gravity within the Democratic Party will most likely have to wait until an open battle for the party nomination.

THE FUTURE OF THE NEW DEMOCRATS

Given the problematic nature of the New Democrats' electoral and policy achievements during the 1990s, what then are their prospects for the future? Clearly, these prospects have diminished greatly now that the Democrats are no longer in control of the White House. Not only have the New Democrats lost control of their most important elected office, but there is little indication that the ideas of the New Democrats constitute a truly transformative political ideology. Such ideologies have in the past realigned the political landscape, fundamentally altering the way in which politics is conducted. Such examples include the rise of the Republican Party in the Civil War era, the development of progressivism in the early part of the twentieth century, the establishment of the New Deal coalition in the 1930s, and the conservative revolution that began with Ronald Reagan.[37]

Why is this the case? Recent writings by Bruce Ackerman are particularly useful here. According to Ackerman, important transformations of American politics have occurred as part of a three-stage process. First, large numbers of Americans have mobilized themselves in social movements with the purpose of changing the political systems. Second, these broad but inchoate social movements have then created or captured a political party, thereby helping to organize the movement and allowing it to capture political power. Third, the leaders of these "movement parties" then used the power of the presidency to transform the political system.[38]

If Ackerman's analysis is correct, the New Democrats are lacking all three conditions. First, despite their efforts, the New Democrats have been unable to develop much in the way of grassroots membership, let alone create a social movement. For the most part, the New Democrats remain limited to a relatively small band of elected officials, political operatives, and intellectuals. Their main institutional entities, the DLC and the Progressive Policy Institute, rely on special interest funding. Finally, the New Democrats actually stand in opposition to many of the core social-movement elements of the Democratic coalition—organized labor, feminists, environmentalists, and civil rights organizations.

Second, the New Democrats lack a strong party organization through which to capture political power. Though the New Democrats have, through Bill Clinton, succeeded in capturing the Democratic Party institutions, in many ways they control a hollow shell. For many years, the capacity of the Democratic Party to organize and mobilize its followers has declined. Furthermore, all "in-parties" suffer, since they are beholden to the interests of their presidents. The Democratic Party under Bill Clinton is no exception to this rule. Indeed, it may have suffered more than other in-parties, since the number of Democratic elected officials in Congress and in state legislatures has declined dramatically. Furthermore, the party apparatus of the Democratic National Committee has suffered as a result of the 1996 Clinton campaign fund-raising scandals.

Finally, though the New Democrats control the presidency, Bill Clinton no longer shows the inclination to be the type of activist president required for movement parties to succeed. After failing in his efforts to reform health care—his one major effort to transform the political and policy landscape—and then being forced to confront a Republican Congress, Clinton has eschewed any broad legislative agenda and has instead chosen to focus on a series of small initiatives, often relying on executive orders or private volunteer efforts to put them into place.[39] Even if this were not the case, Clinton's personal troubles have greatly curtailed his legislative goals, if not his political popularity. In many ways, Clinton's focus on small, nonlegislative programs and private efforts is reminiscent of George H. Bush's call for a "thousands points of light" that would replace large government programs.

NEW DEMOCRATS AND MODERN REPUBLICANS

Rather than the type of transformative ideology described by Ackerman, the New Democrats are more of what I would describe as an *accomodationist* ideology. By this, I mean an ideology that attempts to accommodate itself with the dominant political tides by presenting a more moderate version of the latter. In this way, the New Democrats are akin to the "Modern Republicanism" of the Eisenhower era. This label was used by President Dwight Eisenhower to describe his brand of moderate conservatism. Ike recognized that the New Deal had forever changed American politics and that the Republican Party needed to realize this or pay the price. "Should any political party attempt to abolish Social Security, unemployment insurance, and eliminate labor laws and farm programs," he wrote in 1954, "you would not hear of that party again in our political history."[40] In contrast, Eisenhower tried to rebuild the Republican Party in a more moderate vein, assuring voters that he and other Modern Republicans would not attempt to undermine popular New Deal programs, but only to run them more prudently.

This approach had its successes. Though Eisenhower's status as a war hero made him extremely popular, he was also aided greatly by the perception that he was more moderate than the rest of the GOP. Furthermore, Eisenhower had some significant policy achievements, most notably the construction of the Interstate Highway System and the establishment of federal aid to higher education. But these accomplishments were rather limited in scope. Eisenhower's brand of Modern Republicanism lacked a mass base and thus was unable to transform either the Republican Party or the broader political system. And Ike's policy successes are best seen not as the triumph of Modern Republicanism, but rather as a continuation of the liberal policy impulse that began with the New Deal. Finally, despite Eisenhower's ability to capture the White House, the Republicans failed to win control of Congress after 1954 and in 1958 they suffered a massive loss of forty-seven seats in the House and thirteen in the Senate. Today, Modern Republicanism is an historical footnote; the transformation of the Republican Party and American politics would await the rise of the conservative movement over the next two decades.

The New Democrats resemble the Modern Republicans of the 1950s. Indeed, even Bill Clinton has seen the parallel. "Where are all the Democrats?" Clinton raged at a 1993 cabinet meeting discussing his budget plans. "I hope you're all aware we're all Eisenhower Republicans. We're Eisenhower Republicans here, and we are fighting the Reagan Republicans. We stand for lower deficits and free trade and the bond market." "Isn't that great?" he asked sarcastically.[41]

Beyond the policy similarity, the New Democrats mirror Eisenhower's Modern Republicans ideologically. Though not without political and policy successes, the New Democrats lack the popular base to alter the dominant conservative political ideology. They are thus reduced to splitting the difference with or moderating the more unpopular elements of the conservative agenda. And, like the Modern Republicans, they seem likely to eventually pass from the scene, overtaken by a broader and more original political movement.

NOTES

1. Quoted in Jon F. Hale, "The Making of the New Democrats," *Political Science Quarterly* 110 (Summer 1995 <http://www//epn.org/psq/pshale.html>).

2. Dan Balz, "Democrats Chart the Way Back," *Washington Post*, 19 November, 1984, A1.

3. James R. Dickenson, "Democrats Seek Identity After Loss," *Washington Post*, 17 December 1984, A6.

4. Philip A. Klinkner, *The Losing Parties: Out-Party National Committees, 1956-1993* (New Haven: Yale University Press, 1994), 85–86.

5. Hale, "The Making of the New Democrats."

6. Quoted in Hale, "The Making of the New Democrats."

7. Hale, "The Making of the New Democrats."

8. Hale, "The Making of the New Democrats" and Stanley B. Greenberg, *Middle Class Dreams: The Politics and Power of the New American Majority* (New York: Times Books, 1995), 205–206.

9. Hale, "The Making of the New Democrats."

10. Bill Clinton and Al Gore, *Putting People First: How We All Can Change America* (New York: Times Books, 1992), 226.

11. Paul J. Quirk and Jon K. Dalager, "The Election: A 'New Democrat' and a New Kind of Presidential Campaign," in Michael Nelson, ed., *The Elections of 1992* (Washington, DC: Congressional Quarterly Press, 1993), 78 and Harold W. Stanley and Richard G. Niemi, *Vital Statistics on American Politics* (Washington, DC: Congressional Quarterly Press, 1990), 100.

12. See Morris P. Fiorina, *Retrospective Voting in American National Elections* (New Haven : Yale University Press, 1981), Steven J. Rosenstone,

Forecasting Presidential Elections (New Haven : Yale University Press, 1983), and Michael S. Lewis-Beck and Tom W. Rice, *Forecasting Elections* (Washington, DC: CQ Press, 1992) for an introduction to this literature.

13. Harold W. Stanley and Richard G. Niemi, *Vital Statistics On American Politics, Fourth Edition* (Washington, DC: CQ Press, 1994), 418, 432. Unemployment rates found at the Bureau of Labor Statistics home page <http://www//stats.bls.gov/>.

14. For one example of this thinking, see Mickey Kaus, "They Blew It," *The New Republic*, 5 December, 1994, 14–19.

15. "Bureau of Labor Statistics (BLS) Daily Report," 23 June 1995 and BLS home page (<http://www//stats.bls.gov>).

16. Paul R. Abramson, John H. Aldrich, and David W. Rohde, *Change and Continuity in the 1992 Elections* (Washington, DC: CQ Press), 324.

17. Clyde Wilcox, *The Latest American Revolution?: The 1994 Elections and Their Implications for Governance* (New York: St. Martin's Press, 1995), 9, 19.

18. Ruy A. Teixeira and Joel Rogers, "Who Deserted the Democrats in 1994?" *The American Prospect* 23 (Fall 1995): 73–36 (<http://www//epn.org/prospect/23/23teix.html>).

19. "Voter Turnout Falls Sharply Among the Less Affluent." *The New York Times*, 11 June, 1995: A16.

20. Abramson, Aldrich, and Rohde, 312, 331.

21. Wilcox, 18–19.

22. Philip A. Klinkner, "Court and Country in American Politics: The Democratic Party in 1994," in Philip A. Klinkner, *Midterm: The Elections of 1994* (Boulder, CO: Westview Press, 1996).

23. See Dick Morris, *Behind the Oval Office: Winning the Presidency in the Nineties* (New York: Random House, 1997), 80–85.

24. See E. J. Dionne, *They Only Look Dead: Why Progressives Will Dominate the Next Political Era* (New York: Simon and Schuster, 1996), 259–260.

25. Morris, 207.

26. BLS home page (<http://www//stats.bls.gov/>) and Stanley and Niemi, p. 431.

27. Ruy Teixeira, "Who Joined the Democrats?: Understanding the 1996 Elections" Economic Policy Institute Report, 8 November 1996.

28. This is my own list and though it could reasonably be reduced or expanded, I think it provides a fair representation of the policy achievements of the Clinton administration.

29. See Ronald D. Elving, *Conflict and Compromise: How Congress Makes the Law* (New York: Simon and Schuster, 1995).

30. David R. Mayhew, "The Return to Unified Party Control Under Clinton: How Much of a Difference in Lawmaking?" in Bryan D. Jones, *The New American Politics: Reflections on Political Change and the Clinton Administration* (Boulder, CO: Westview Press, 1995), 116–117.

31. Steven Waldman, *The Bill: How the Adventures of Clinton's National Service Bill Reveal What Is Corrupt, Comic, Cynical—and Noble—About Washington* (New York: Viking, 1995) and "Congress Boosts AmeriCorps by $18 Million," Corporation for National Service news release, 21 October 1998.

32. Ruy Teixeira, "Waitress Moms and Technician Dads: The Story Behind the 1998 Election Results," Economic Policy Institute Briefing Paper, 5 November 1998.

33. Thomas B. Edsall, "The Special Interest Gambit," *The Washington Post*, 3 January 1993, C1 and Tom Rosenstiel, *Strange Bedfellows: How Television and the Presidential Candidates Changed American Politics, 1992* (New York: Hyperion, 1994), 281.

34. Noah Isackson, "Demand Grows for Basic Needs," *Chicago Tribune*, 11 December 1997, 7; Dennis O'Brien, "City's 30 Shelters Filled to Capacity," *Baltimore Sun*, 5 December 1997, 1B; Laura Griffin, "New Charities Puts Focus on Emergency Aid Agencies," *Dallas Morning News*, 27 November 1997, 1.

35. The relationship between racism and public attitudes toward welfare is clearly and convincingly demonstrated in Martin Gilens, *Why Americans Hate Welfare: Race, Media, and the Politics of Antipoverty Policy* (Chicago: University of Chicago Press, 1999).

36. Robert Greenstein, Richard Kogan, and Marion Nichols, "Bearing Most of the Burden: How Deficit Reduction During the 104th Congress Concentrated on Programs for the Poor," Center on Budget and Policy Priorities, 3 December 1996 and Robert Greenstein, "Looking at the Details of the New Budget Legislation: Social Program Initiatives Decline Over Time While Upper-Income Tax Cuts Grow," Center on Budget and Policy Priorities, 12 August 1997.

37. James L. Sundquist's, *Dynamics of the Party System: Alignment and Realignment of Political Parties in the United States*, Revised Edition (Washington, DC: Brookings Institution, 1983) provides a useful analysis of political and ideological realignments in American history.

38. Bruce Ackerman, "The Broken Engine of Progressive Politics," *The American Prospect*, 38 (May–June 1998): 34-43 (<http://www.epn.org/prospect/ 38/38ackefs.html>).

39. James Bennett and Robert Pear, "Clinton's Little Initiatives Lead to Substantial Changes in Some Areas," *New York Times*, 8 December 1997, A1.

40. Stephen E. Ambrose, *Eisenhower*, vol. II, *The President* (New York: Simon and Schuster, 1984), 219.

41. Bob Woodward, *The Agenda: Inside the Clinton White House* (New York: Simon and Schuster, 1994), 165.

7

Political Parties and Democracy's Citizens

Stephen F. Schneck

resently, American political parties have reached a point of crisis that revolves around a two-sided paradox. That paradox concerns the role of political parties for citizenship. Indeed, the crisis is obvious in the playing out of the paradox, such that, *on one hand*, by nearly every conceivable measure political parties appear to be withering in general. While, *on the other*, within the diminishing rump of political parties, there is evidence of an inflamed stridency associated with narrow interests and passionate activism. Illuminated from these perspectives, the theoretical paradox of political parties and democracy's citizens is revealed. Revealed also is the peculiar American history of this paradox in our party and governmental system.

Age-old political thinking has it that participatory forms of government require remarkable citizens. Moreover, all the classical takes on democracy, from Aristotle to Montesquieu, agree that these needed "good citizens" are not born or found. Likewise, the argument runs, good citizens do not spring full grown from their private lives and they do not emerge complete from that nonpolitical, quasi-public sphere we call "society." Instead, the old theories claim, they are "cultivated" in unique, public, political spaces wherein they acquire the virtues, knowledge, and pragmatism necessary for good citizenship. In this vein, the concern of this chapter is to consider what political parties should mean for democracy's "good citizens." Partly, too, the chapter will consider what democracy would be with such citizens and such political parties. And, partly, in conclusion, the chapter will appraise the distance between the political parties of the United

States and the criteria for the sort of political parties found to be conducive to citizenship and democracy. But, first, there is the theoretical paradox noted in regard to citizenship and democracy that will serve to frame any discussion of American political parties and American citizenship.

The paradox is about the irony of "cultivating" citizens. For, to the extent that the process of cultivation determines the qualities and exercise of citizenship, it threatens the basic promise of legitimacy in a democracy—i.e., that the citizens are sovereign and should govern as they freely *choose* to govern. Taken to extremes, the "cultivation" of citizens (so prized by classical analysis of democracy) imperils democracy's theoretical foundation in free and diverse popular sovereignty, yielding instead a dubious homogeneity among the citizenry.

Anticipating his own later thinking about the role of political parties for addressing this paradox, James Madison spoke to both the need for special citizens and the dilemma of their cultivation in his famed Federalist #10. Left to themselves, he reasoned, democratic subjects would succumb to their self-interests and narrow passions. "So strong is this propensity of mankind," he wrote, "that where no substantial occasion presents itself, the most frivolous and fanciful distinctions have been sufficient to kindle unfriendly passions and excite their most violent conflicts."[1] Common public enterprises could not succeed in a politics divided by such passions and interests. People, in other words, must be brought into political participation in a manner that allows them to rise above private interests so as to provide for good citizenship.

Cognizant of the paradox, however, Madison noted that many efforts to resolve the cancer of private passions could well be "worse than the disease." Cultivation of democracy's needed good citizenship must not endanger either the liberty to make political choices nor the differences among choices that make liberty valuable. For, he claimed, "the protection of these faculties is the first object of government."[2] To resolve the paradox, Madison reasoned, some means must be devised that encourages citizenship to stand above narrow passions—but, at the same time does not imperil the theoretical necessity for citizen liberty and difference. Where do political parties, especially American political parties, fit into this reasoning?

The literature of political and other social sciences is *not* wonderfully helpful in assessing the relationships among parties, citizenship, and democracy.[3] Only in a limited way has modern social science explored the relationship. Max Weber, Roberto Michels, Robert Dahl, and many others writing of the importance of political parties for participatory government *have* discussed, if only tangentially, a role for parties in "developing" an electorate capable of participatory government. Likewise, in the specialized political science literature on political parties, authors such as Maurice Duverger and Giovanni Sartori have made much of the "educative" function of parties in democracies, but have offered little discussion of this "education" in terms of the paradox of remarkable citizens. Unfortunately, "education" and "development" in the social science literature are usually explained in terms like disseminating information and voter mobilization. Berelson, Lazarsfeld, and McPhee's well-known study of the irony of democratic citizenship, *Voting*, for example, treats parties' function as drawing together the four elements needed by democracy's citizens: knowledge, participation, rationality, and individualism.[4]

But, implicitly these investigations by contemporary political science, nevertheless, *do* support what the classical authors stated forthrightly—that democratic citizenship requires mortgaging private interests for the commonweal, without which the centrifugal tendencies of private interests would overwhelm the political order. And, although the paradox of political parties and democracy's citizens is seldom addressed directly, it might well be argued that that same paradox is located very near the center of the crisis of American political parties today, where from one perspective political scientists observe parties dealigning into unremarkable, and perhaps apathetic, individualism and from another perspective are suborned by intense, narrow, and passionate factions. For, as evidenced in the analyses of many of the other authors in this volume, political science has become aware that contemporary American political parties are increasingly failing to provide for the remarkable citizens that democracy needs. "Remarkable," in this sense, refers not so much to a citizen who is knowledgeable, rational, participatory, and individual. Instead, it refers more to a citizen who can transcend narrow, detached self-interests and factional passions, while avoiding the imposition of someone's version of a monolithic "common good" that would foreclose the liberty and difference that are the promise and legitimation of democracy. Arguably, elements of such thinking were part of the intellectual milieu from which emerged history's first political parties in the United States.

CITIZENSHIP AND DEMOCRACY

The origin of the United States' government is also the origin of history's first political parties. Nascent political parties are evident in the ratification debates surrounding the 1787 Constitution, parties that can be called the Federalists and the Anti-Federalists. These "proto-parties" demonstrated the curious amalgam of the pragmatic and the ideological, as well as the national and the regional, that has come to be regarded as the earmark of American political parties. More importantly, it should be remembered that the principal division between the Federalist proponents of the Constitution and their Anti-Federalist opponents was one that turned on the question of citizenship in participatory government. Central to the Constitutional debate, in other words, was the question of democracy and its citizens.

Scholars today agree that it was the Anti-Federalists who were more classical in their understanding of democracy and its needed citizens.[5] With Aristotle, and especially with Montesquieu, the Anti-Federalists believed that participatory government would work only with strong civic virtue. Civic virtue provided the centripetal gravity required to balance the centrifugal effects of politics based upon individual rights and liberties. Inculcation of virtues that celebrated republican duty, patriotism, and communal affection served to moderate the divisiveness of a politics where sovereignty was divided inherently among the many individual citizens.

It was believed by the Anti-Federalists that such civic virtue was to be had only in a unique setting. That setting is one familiar to students of ancient studies of democracy. The setting desired by the Anti-Federalists included: small, discrete communities with geographical boundaries; communities with a population homogenous in terms of values and sentiments; communities of relative equality; and communities of shared interests. The political position of the Anti-Federalists makes sense in this light. They favored the local over the national. They stressed the need to preserve parochial sentiments in the face of national interests. They strongly advocated the importance of religion for democracy while simultaneously demanding a bill of rights that protected the religious practices of local communities from intrusions by either the national state or from intense national majorities. They feared a national military while advocating the duty of citizens to bear arms and to participate in local militias.

Quoting from Montesquieu, the Anti-Federalist "Brutus" notes that "in a large republic, the public good is sacrificed to a thousand views; it is subordinate to exceptions, and depends on accidents. In a small one, the interest of the public is easier perceived, better understood, and more within the reach of every citizen; abuses are of less extent, and of course are less protected." He continues . . .

> In a republic, the manners, sentiments, and interests of the people should be similar. If this not be the case, there will be a constant clashing of opinions; and the representatives of one part will be continually striving against those of the other. This will retard the operation of government, and prevent such conclusions as will promote the public good.[6]

Without such conditions, the Anti-Federalists reasoned, civic virtue would be impossible and participatory government would not work. With their affection for local religious communities and small, agrarian towns, the Anti-Federalists obviously liked intense communities of public interest for their ability to provide for such civic virtue in citizens.

Their Federalist opponents, however, thought quite differently about these matters. They placed a greater premium on individual liberty and difference, and they feared the smothering effect of intense communities. For this reason, where the Anti-Federalists sought to make participatory government work *internally*, by educating the hearts and souls of citizens through civic virtue, their Federalist opponents sought to achieve the same result *externally*, by placing limits on anarchical or tyrannical extremes of citizen behavior through laws enforced by the superior power of a central government. As one well-known scholar of the period puts it:

It is no surprise that the framers rejected the classical case for the small state. Madison was hostile to the "spirit of locality" in general, not only in the states. Small communities afford the individual less power, less mastery, and, hence, less liberty than do large states. Moreover, the small community lays hold of the affections of the individual and leads him to accept the very restraints on his interest and liberty that are inherent in smallness. The classics urged the small state in part because it might encourage the individual to limit and rule his private passions. Madison rejected such states because he rejected that sort of restraint. Small communities limit opportunities and meddle with the soul.[7]

There is an Hobbesian ambiance about Federalist thinking. The Federalists judged that the political community was incapable of overcoming selfish passions and individual interests. The pursuit of such passions and interests would derive inevitably from the free choices of citizens with sufficient liberty. For the Anti-Federalists' solution to work, Madison argued in Federalist #10, it would require a civic virtue that overwhelmed liberty itself—and that was too high a price for obtaining citizen rule. For Federalists, "the first object of government" was preserving "the diversity of faculties among men."[8] The ancient (and Anti-Federalist) thinking that democracies required a common good inculcated by civic virtue endangered this "first object."

Overt, lawlike constraints on the democratic spirit—enforced by the coercive power of government—were preferable to the tacit and insidious mechanisms of civic virtue. Laws and similar formal procedures are promulgated widely, are subject to deliberation and public review, and are thus *objects* exterior to the sensibilities that are then able to be accepted or resisted in the minds and hearts of citizens. Exterior constraints, furthermore, create walls of an arena within which pluralism and citizen difference are granted "free" expression. The Federalists wanted exactly this.

At the heart of such reasoning is a pragmatic appreciation of pluralism and liberty. Anticipating the utilitarianism of the political economists and drawing from the same Scottish Enlightenment sources that inspired them, Federalists wished to design a system of competing selfish passions such that a transcendent political rationality would result. As reasoned in a well-known phrase, "ambition must be made to counteract ambition."[9] From the interplay of many differing and conflicting individual interests and passions, checked only in the extreme by efficacious laws, they believed, results an harmonious calculus. Those same individualized passions that otherwise may endanger a republic are regulated by their own competition such that the system itself is rational and ordered.[10]

There is a kinship here, too, with the utilitarian notion of the free market of ideas. Good policy will out, thought many Federalists, from the interplay of free individuals each engaged in the pursuit of self-interest. The state succeeds by promoting and protecting the diversity of interests and the liberty of individual citizens. Civic virtue here would be limited to rather thin and procedural values like tolerance and civility. The Federalists defended the seemingly undemocratic aspects of their 1787 constitution as necessary mechanisms for promoting the balancing of interests by which they understood the spirit of democracy itself.[11] By protecting the competition of self-interests, government would be protecting the very motor of civilization and of responsible politics. Federalist #10, again, is illustrative. Where classical theories of democracy argued for elimination or domination of factional interests, understanding them to be perils to democracy, the Federalists did not wish to destroy factions. They wanted a system of myriad competing factions designed to foster permanent competition. The system of competition itself, moreover, would achieve a rationality that could not be attained by passion-blinded human beings themselves.

Although their two positions have been somewhat exaggerated in the foregoing for rhetorical consistency, it is fair to say that the two proto-parties, the Anti-Federalists and the Federalists, clearly conceived distinct means for making participatory government viable. An emphasis on the possibility of the common good (for the local community) and civic virtue were the Anti-Federalists' preferred mechanisms. Competing self-interests and active government were preferred by the Federalists. Their preferences, moreover, suggest different notions of citizenship for each. The *Federalist* citizen, it seems, would be autonomous, self-reliant, and privately directed. No special public spaces are required for the cultivation of citizenship. Federalist citizens, in contrast with ancient ideas about citizenship for democracies, would emerge complete as political actors from their private lives without any role for the political community. Individuals' participation in public affairs, as human activity generally, would reflect self-interest.

The *Anti-Federalist* conception, in contrast, has citizenship as some kind of goal for which ongoing cultivation within a small-scale political setting is necessary. In this conception, one is gradually trained and directed by the political community toward good citizenship. Training directs sentiments to consider the common good, emphasizing loyalty, duty, and sacrifice. Citizenship is defined by reference to one's place in the community and to the responsibility that such place entails. As did the Federalists, the Anti-Federalists stressed liberty but for them liberty was not the absence of obligations beyond self-interest. Indeed, their thinking suggests a belief that the obligations of citizenship are the conditions of liberty.

These notions of citizenship that lie beneath the thinking of the Federalists and the Anti-Federalists may seem far removed from present concerns about the function and responsibilities of political parties in the United States. Yet, history's first political parties were birthed in the debates surrounding these old notions. Throughout the political history of the United States, the differences here have gradually resolved themselves into a party system that largely represents what has here been associated with the "Federalist" apology for the Constitution.[12]

The term "Federalist," in this sense, refers only to the ratification period. It must not be confused directly with the political party of Adams and Hamilton. It refers instead to the curious fit between the minds of Madison and Hamilton that found such remarkable expression in the apologies they penned with other "Federalists" in support of the 1787 Constitution. Indeed, the divisions that subsequently emerged in the first government were largely divisions *within* "Federalist" thinking. John Adams and Alexander Hamilton emphasized the constitutional demand for a large-scale national system and vigorous government. Thomas Jefferson and James Madison emphasized the idea of interests in competition. It is as if the Jeffersonian Republicans and the Federalists divided the legacy of "Federalist" thinking between them. *Anti-Federalist* thinking, however, does not simply disappear. In Adams' frequent appeal to civic virtue and in Jefferson's obvious affection for local community, the political thought of the

Anti-Federalists found some small footholds in both of the early political parties—albeit more comfortably with the Jeffersonians. Nonetheless, the history of political thought in American politics reveals a pattern of weaning from the concerns of the Anti-Federalists. "Federalist" thinking triumphs in the combining and recombining of its basic elements over the two centuries of American politics. As this way of thinking and practicing has triumphed, however, it has brought American political parties (and with them the legitimacy of the republic) to a point where the paradox of political parties and democracy's citizens is again palpable.

POLITICAL PARTIES

Not surprisingly, considering what has been said, Anti-Federalist thinking would likely be more conducive for the formation of political parties than would Federalist. The greater attention to community and group, the corresponding appreciation of loyalty and duty, suggest an affinity in Anti-Federalist thought for something like the idea of parties. European political parties as well as similarly styled political parties elsewhere around the globe suggest, further, that political parties themselves can be effective instruments for developing civic virtue among citizens. And, of course, the powerful focus on local communities in Anti-Federalist thinking coincides with "grassroots" politics, where political parties have traditionally had greatest salience.

Federalist thinking, on the other hand, is much less conducive for political parties. Citizens organizing to intervene in the policy-making process is viewed with suspicion. Factions and groups are inevitably cause for concern inasmuch as they are potentially dangerous concentrations of human passions. Even an organization that formed a political majority, Madison thought, would reflect only the irrational sentiments of its adherents and, hence, would forever threaten tyranny to a republic. Human organizations (groups, religions, communities, factions, and—likely—parties) could never achieve the rationality necessary for responsible government. Only the system of free and open competition in pursuit of self-interest could hold out that hope. Political parties, it seems, would surely skew the needed free interplay of such a system. Much like the manner in which economists see oligopolies distorting the correct operation of a free-enterprise market, Federalist thinking might well perceive political parties as organizing passions and interests into blocs that foreclose the desired openness and competition, thereby distorting legitimate outcomes. Political parties, factions, and similar groups, further, would weaken the national character of the political system by dividing the whole against itself. This picture is reflected in the Federalists' fears of local loyalties and of all loyalties based on distinctions of ethnicity, religion, language, and culture.[13] Political parties, therefore, because they might reflect such parochial loyalties, because they may distort the competition of self-interests, and because they cannot achieve rationality in politics, do not seem well suited to the Federalist understanding of workable, participatory government.

Why, then, did political parties arise in the midst of Federalist thinking? William N. Chambers in his excellent studies of the origin of political parties in America contends that the explanation is twofold: pragmatic and theoretical.[14] The first political party, the Jeffersonian-Republican, was organized by the nature of its opposition to policies of Alexander Hamilton and John Adams. That is, Chambers argues, the first political party, formed not to govern or to pursue office, but instead to provide rationale and organization to those in opposition to the existing government. All of which inclined the government, in turn, to organize its own supporters in response. Chambers goes on to note, more importantly, that both political parties saw their formation as something of a response to the intense smaller scale political cliques and intrigues that had arisen in the state governments under the Articles of Confederation and into the early years of the new republic. Fitting this into "Federalist thinking," it can be supposed that both political parties feared the passionate sentiments of these small-scale factions and welcomed national political parties as somewhat more bloodless organizations that were able to co-opt and transcend narrow passions. Amorphous, national political parties, in this sense, would be seen as a far lesser evil than the intensely unified factions that might be organized on the basis of localism, religion, ethnicity, ideology, or the like.

From these roots in Federalist thinking can be traced an important line in the history of American political parties. While there are obvious anomalies (like the Jacksonian Democrats, the Populists, and city machines) the history of political parties bears the imprint of its origin. Through reform after reform, through the rise and fall of the various parties themselves, through Civil War, Reconstruction, and Progressivism, it is Federalist thinking that outs. The picture of political parties today reveals this. They are loose, national coalitions of interests that have limited meaning beyond their pragmatic electoral efforts. The American citizenry, when polled, admits to finding the whole idea of political parties a troublesome one.[15] American political parties are not "corporate" in the way that factions or groups or communities seem to be. Ideologically, they are not cohesive—nor, increasingly, are they cohesive in efforts at governing or making policy (although one might argue that they remain somewhat cohesive "negatively" within government, as opponents to policy making). One well-known political scientist calls American political parties "labels," as if there were nothing beneath the name itself. Indeed, over the history of the republic, and despite occasional moves to the contrary, even American efforts to reform the party system show a pattern in keeping with Federalist thinking. From caucuses to conventions to primaries, the pattern is one of increasing emphasis on citizens engaged in a marketlike, open process of competition for self-interest. Likewise, intense narrow loyalties are discouraged in favor of a thin, national, electroal focus.

Recent studies of American voters and parties, by and large, support such analysis. James Ceaser's *Presidential Selection* traces at the presidential level a history of political parties over two hundred years wherein republican restraint gives way to interest competition. Political parties, Ceaser argues, have become national instruments for mass aggregation of individual and group interests. Ceaser correctly associates this trend with the Progressive movement in American politics, but fails to discover the link between the Progressives he disdains and the Framers he reveres.[16] James Sundquist's *Dynamics of the Party System*, unlike Ceaser, identifies the linkage between the "progressive" reforms of political parties and the intent of Framers like Madison.[17] Sundquist, however, celebrates this move of political parties toward a marketlike understanding of democracy and citizenship based upon competitive self-interests. Kevin Phillips, in his *Post-Conservative America*, follows a similar line through history, coming close to saying that the Reagan years were an aberration in a long trend toward what has here been called "Federalist thinking." Citing what he calls "mediacracy," "plebiscitary parties," and "supraparty coalitions," Phillips traces a fifty-year pattern of political parties that points toward a future that plainly embodies the Federalist vision.

> What we'll probably see are short-term political coalitions and supremacies based more on communication technology than on old-style parties. In the process, our politics will become increasingly prone to plebiscitary techniques and appeals. The American party system seems a long way from overcoming weakness. In fact, that weakness is probably moving front and center.[18]

Written in 1983, long before Perot and Clinton and before the vaunted "third way" promoted by contemporary politicians from Gerhard Schroeder and Tony Blair to Al Gore and John McCain, Kevin Phillips must be quite pleased with his reasoning here.

But, the withering of American political parties on the macro scale is only half of the story. For, parties are *not* being replaced with greater and more thoughtful individual participation in the political process. Democracy's needed "remarkable" citizens have *not* emerged to occupy the place vacated by political parties. Instead, the political landscape left behind by the retreating political parties resembles nothing so much as the dystopia of factionalism that Madison feared in Federalist #10. Narrow, often single-issue, factions are multiplying within policy-making and campaigning circles. Moreover, while pragmatism is still common among these factions, there is an increasingly feverish ideological character appearing as well. So, on one hand, citizens in general are opting out of regular, organized, and dutiful participation in politics—evidenced by low voter turnout, disgust with politics, diminished involvement in civic duties, and declining interest in public affairs. Yet, on the other hand, "inside the Beltway" and within focused, smaller, and often interest-driven groups around the country, emotions, ideological fervor, and passionate political participation are high by historical measure. Political parties are being replaced by what Madison surely would have called "factions." And, these factions comprise a curious combination of strident, ideological activists joined with *Realpolitik* professionals and experts.

It seems fair to say that, while the Federalists and the Anti-Federalists never anticipated the emergence of political parties, they plainly anticipated (and worried about) factions. The eminent political scientist, Robert Dahl, for example, reads Madison's Federalist #10 as promoting a system of factions in competition.[19] In Dahl's assessment, the Federalists acknowledged not only the inevitability of factions, but also their *necessity* for participatory, republican government. When Madison wrote, then, of the value of the size of the proposed republic, according to Dahl, the advantage was that the scope of the new republic allowed the competition of interests to occur not only among individuals but also among interest groups. Dahl draws inspiration from this curious reading of Federalist thinking and he evidences a great appreciation of the policy-making interdependency that has emerged over the last thirty years involving interest groups, elected government representatives, and nonelected government officers and staff. Although stridently critical of the "undemocratic" aspects of this system as it now works, Dahl is in conformity with his reading of Federalist thinking about its possibilities for government. He is led to argue for the unique legitimacy of policies arrived at in the competition among the clusters of interest both in and out of government. Called *polyarchy* by Dahl, the Federalist-inspired theory is perhaps better named by critics, like Ted Lowi, who call it "interest group liberalism."[20]

In many ways, the reading of Federalist thinking offered in this chapter parallels Dahl's. Different, though, is its reading of what the Federalist thinking portends for the present and future of American political parties and democracy's needed citizens. Dahl, too, finds a legacy from Federalist thinking in the role of interest groups (or factions) for contemporary government and politics. Yet, he understands the presence and activity of these factions in contemporary politics as part of the genius of the Federalist response to the paradox of democracy's citizens. An argued advantage of the Constitution, according to the Federalists and Dahl, is its ability to make use of factions. Keeping such groups small enough so as to guard against the tyranny of any single concentration of interests, while simultaneously drawing on the passions and intensity of such groups for driving policy making, was championed by the Federalists as an inherent virtue of the constitutional government. Political parties of the bloodless, dispassionate sort preferred in the fashion developed from Federalist thought would only enhance the ability of the republic to make use of factions via a system of countervailing competition. Thus, factions are in keeping with the Federalist legacy in American intellectual history. But, the Federalist-inspired notion of political parties is a necessary remedy to dissipate the dangerous energy and passions such factions generate. The kicker is, though, that the remedy of Federalist-inspired political parties has itself unfolded in American history and political practices in a way that has resulted in political parties unable to perform their needed function.

Dahl's own concerns about the direct and autonomous access that contemporary factions have to government speaks to this, and reveals his sympathy for the Federalists—especially Madison—as well as his sympathy for "thin" political parties. The triumph of factionalism, besides diminishing the role for political parties in making policy, poses a danger to republican government itself. Both Hamilton and Madison worried about the entrée of intense human passions into government. Such passions can wither the rationality achieved by deliberation, compromise, and the checks and balances of competing ambitions. Hence, it seems more in keeping with Federalist thought that the steadier and more reasoned presence of political parties should serve as a buffer between the passions of interests—in groups or otherwise—and participatory government.

There is an irony in this concern for deliberateness and rationality. For, owing to their bleak appraisal of human nature, the Federalists hold out no hope that such qualities can ever be fostered among the citizens themselves. The political system of the republic itself can be engineered for rationality and deliberateness, the Federalists thought, but citizens could never be brought by dint of civic virtue to this maturity. Political parties, it is supposed, as partial versions of the national arena of competition, might bring some measure of rationality to politics by balancing the passions and interests of their members, thereby cooling narrow passions and interests as they interact and are co-opted into larger alliances. Such political parties could replace mature, deliberate, and remarkable citizens (the sort democracy needs) with a mature and deliberate *process*, the effects of which would substitute for remarkable citizenship.

POLITICAL PARTIES AND CITIZENSHIP

Where, then, have things gone awry? How is it that the Federalist thinking that gave us our political parties has now also brought us to the present crisis? The answer, arguably, turns on the Federalist effort to replace remarkable citizenship with a remarkable process.

Indeed, is it any wonder, given their provenance, that present-day political parties in the United States fail to provide settings for the cultivation of the remarkable citizens needed for responsible democracy? As the exemplars of Federalist thinking, political parties function to enforce a vision of politics based upon interests in competition. Far from endeavoring to direct members toward public-regarding virtues, political parties are unable even to effect electoral discipline among their members in office. Citing classical political thinkers and examples from the history of republics and democracies, the Anti-Federalists offered telling pictures of the inevitable dissolution of such governments when stripped of their necessary, remarkable citizens.

For example, the Anti-Federalist "Impartial Examiner" predicted a dissolute future for a republic based upon Federalist thinking. This dissolution of the republic would not be soon, the Examiner thought, since "it is nearly impossible to enslave a people immediately after a firm struggle against oppression, while the sense of past injury is recent." Such struggle, it is supposed, engenders precisely the public-regarding civic virtue necessary for cultivating good citizens. No, the dissolution would come much later when "the altar of liberty is no longer watched with such assiduity," when "a new train of passions succeeds to the empire of the mind," and when "the charms of which arose from the *republican plan*, insensibly decline." Mentioning "prosperity, voluptuousness, excessive fondness for riches, and luxury," the Examiner claimed that a "fatal avenue" for the republic would be opened.

The implication was that the Federalists did not appreciate that their own thinking depended on an underlying civic virtue and concern for the common good that issued from the Revolution. As that memory dwindled, the underlying foundation eroded as private interest crowded out other concerns in politics.

> Hence, it follows, that in the midst of this general contageon
> [*sic*] a few men—or one—more powerful than all the others,

industriously endeavor to obtain all authority; and perhaps by
means of great wealth—or embezzling the public money,—
perhaps totally subvert the government and erect a system of
aristocratic or monarchic tyranny in its room.[21]

This replays the classical portrayal of the devolution of democracy.
Without civic virtue, citizens become privately regarding. This saps
the possibility of consensus from democratic politics, resulting in policy-
making stagnation or anarchy. Citizens then begin to consider the
demagogues that always plague participatory government and begin
to heed those who promise miraculous solutions to their policy-
making problems (in return, always, for citizens surrendering their authority and responsibility). As Aristotle had argued, democracies without
remarkable citizens are followed by tyrants. The Impartial Examiner
faulted the Federalists and their new Constitution for failing to consider
this propensity in participatory government and its citizens.

> It is this deprivation of manners, this wicked propensity, my
> dear countrymen, against which you ought to provide with
> the utmost degree of prudence and circumspection. All re-
> publican nations pass this *parokism [sic]* of vice at some pe-
> riod or other;—and if at that dangerous juncture your
> government is not secure upon a solid foundation, and well
> guarded against the machinations of evil men, the liberties of
> this country will be lost—perhaps forever.[22]

If the Anti-Federalist fears for the republic are accurate, then concern
is warranted for the increasing failure of the republic to provide for
public, political settings (in political parties or elsewhere) that would
enable the formation of the sorts of citizens democracy needs.

This is not to say, however, that the Anti-Federalists and their
classical inspiration offer a conception of citizenship, and with it a role
for political parties, that is entirely preferable to Federalist thinking.
Far from it. Indeed, while Federalist thinking errs by providing no
space for arriving at genuine citizenship by filling such space with
private interests, Anti-Federalist thinking (not so paradoxically) might
well close off such space with an enforced, singular model of citizenship. For the civic virtue prized by ancient democrats and Anti-Federalists (and prized today, it seems, by many critics of contemporary

American politics) leans perilously in the direction of eliminating the "diversity of faculties among men" that Madison correctly saw as essential for the free exercise of political choice and that forms the media for responsible citizenship. There is, then, a curiously anti-democratic bent to those theories of democracy that would homogenize human minds and hearts so that such participatory government would be tranquil and ordered. Whatever political parties should mean for citizenship, for example, they should not constrain the pluralism and diversity of citizens, which lie so close to the font of political responsibility.

So, if today's political parties are to contribute toward democracy's remarkable citizens—and if they are not to copy the ancients in this by merely enforcing a static, singular civic virtue upon their membership—then how are they to achieve this? Again, but now with some wariness considering its dangers, some answer might be found in Anti-Federalist thinking. Not in those Anti-Federalist and ancient hopes at fostering an overwhelming, singular civic virtue, but rather in the Anti-Federalist defense of localism against the national republic can be found a glimpse of what role political parties might play for democracy's citizens.

For the Anti-Federalist affection for local communities was not merely a romantic agrarianism, nor was it merely expedient politics. The stress on the importance of diverse, local communities was also theoretical. The vitality and political power of such communities, they thought, was crucial to the preservation of liberty. They thought that local communities served as *barriers* to any singular power that the national republic might exercise over its citizens. Local loyalties would strive against national loyalties, dividing citizens' hearts. Such division itself worked to check and diminish the strength of the national grip. As a barrier to the formation of powerful ties to the national republic, then, local communities would protect the liberty of citizens to act responsibly in politics. In playing national loyalties against state and local ones, the Anti-Federalists sought to maximize citizen opportunities for developing the citizenship that participatory government required. Equally, defending localism also defended diversity and pluralism in the regime itself. The Bill of Rights that was demanded by the Anti-Federalists, was not written to guarantee the rights of individuals *per se*. The Anti-Federalists' proposal did not reflect the idea of universal "rights of man" that were then being trumpeted by the French *philosophes* in anticipation of the 1789 revolution. Rather, and quite differently, the proposed Bill of Rights exemplified the Anti-Federalist concern for protecting diverse, local communities from the potentially homogenizing power of the national state, understood not only governmentally but also in a broader sense of politics. In this way, local communities could provide diverse public spaces, in their differing political environments, for the formation of remarkable citizens.

CONCLUSION

Wrestling with the paradox of political parties and democracy's citizens, I agreed with James Madison at the beginning of this chapter, requires some means by which citizens might stand above their self-interested passions while at the same time not sacrificing their liberty, diversity, or participation in the public life of their community. Yet, the idea (the Federalist idea) of political parties as it has developed in American history and political practice has fallen short on both counts. On one side, the role of political parties is being taken by narrower factions organized around self-interested passion. On the other side, citizen participation has declined and the appreciation of meaningful differences in public policies—the diversity of faculties that lends liberty its savor—has eroded.

The present crisis of political parties reveals this reality starkly. Zealous and passionate insiders dominate the rump of political parties that survives. At the same time, to the average American, political parties' differences are of little salience. Citizens, save for the insiders, less and less feel efficacy or meaningful attachment with their political parties. They reason that their participation is marginalized if it does not conform with the zealots and rendered meaningless if it does.

Would that the crisis of contemporary political parties were only that. Because, not only does the present reality of American political parties work against the possibility of effective political parties themselves—not only, in other words, do parties fail to support the development of the needed remarkable citizens—their crisis also abets and intensifies the erosion of such citizenship as still exists. The crisis of political parties in this regard points in the direction of a possible larger crisis—a crisis of legitimacy—wherein the question of citizen rule itself becomes central. Sovereign citizenship wanes; nonparticipating, self-interested public opinion waxes; and the ranks of activists, professionals, and experts wax even more.

Rethinking the role for political parties and democracy's citizens brings much of this into relief. A differently constituted political party system can be imagined, one derived perhaps from a careful reading of the Anti-Federalists while informed with an awareness of Madison's paradox. Parties, in such a system, would be locations for public-spirited contention and discourse, places wherein the diversity of ideas can be played out and appreciated, and places where citizens would join with others to deliberate, question, and propose that which concerns matters of public life. The remarkable citizenship needed by democracy might well be nourished in such settings.

What this would mean in practice is harder to picture. Of course, political parties need to become the primary vehicle for citizens' participation in their political life. Surely, too, such participation would need to encompass far more than voting and elections. One might imagine meaningful opportunities to deliberate, learn, listen to others, propose policies, and thus mature as remarkable citizens. Drawing from local inspiration and diverse public-spirited voices, parties might be reconstituted as instruments for exercising popular sovereignty, neutering and displacing today's activists and experts.

POST-ELECTION ADDENDUM

The descriptions of crisis and paradox seem even more salient from a vantage point of just days after the Supreme Court ruled in favor of George W. Bush to end the 2000 election. Much has been made comparing recent events with the Hayes/Tilden election of 1876. Then, however, the nation was truly and bitterly divided by the aftermath of Civil War and punitive Reconstruction. No such powerful division exists in the electorate today. Low voter turnout and much polling about issues are telling on this matter. Yet, in regard to the Florida ballot controversies, a minority of activists, issue advocates, and "professional" political workers invoked among themselves a depth of partisan rancor unmatched in recent memory. Most Americans do not care for political parties, but an inside minority has become passionately zealous. Given democracy's need for citizens to be able to mortgage self-interest in favor of citizenship and public duty, neither the complacency of the majority nor the rancor of the minority are encouraging.

Similarly, a political solution to the Florida situation was rejected in favor of a curious, nonpolitical process that emphasized the expertise of professionals and the passion of activists. A political solution (perhaps revolving around the Florida legislature and the Congress) likely would have demanded that elected officials and their parties shoulder full responsibility. Citizens—within their respective political parties—would weigh the actions of their representatives. Instead, the process went to pundits, to interest groups, to professionally organized "political" theater, and ultimately to the courts.

NOTES

1. Federalist #10, from Alexander Hamilton, John Jay, and James Madison, *The Federalist: A Commentary on the Constitution of the United States; Being a Collection of Essays Written in Support of the Constitution agreed upon September 17, 1787, by the Federal Convention.* (hereafter Federalist) (New York: Modern Library, 1947) 56.

2. Federalist #10, p 55.

3. Perhaps an exception to this sweeping generalization is M. Ostrogorski's *Democracy and the Organization of Political Parties* (New York: Reeve's, 1902). Although Ostrogorski does not understand citizenship in the classical manner, he clearly does recognize it to involve a profound normative component.

4. Bernard R. Berelson, Paul F. Lazarsfeld, and William McPhee. *Voting.* (Chicago: University of Chicago Press, 1954).

5. See, for example, Herbert Storing's book, *What the Anti-Federalists Were For* (Chicago: University of Chicago Press, 1981), 73–6.

6. Brutus {Robert Yates?}, Letter I, *New York Journal*, 18 October, 1787. From *The Essential Antifederalist*, eds. W. B. Allen and Gordon Lloyd (Washington D.C.: UPA, 1985), 107, 109.

7. Wilson Carey McWilliams, "Democracy and the Citizen: Community Dignity, and the Crisis of Contemporary Politics in America," in *How Democratic is the Constitution?* eds. Robert A. Goldwin and William A. Schambra (Washington: AEI, 1980), 89.

8. Federalist #10.

9. Federalist #51.

10. The author has argued elsewhere that the marketlike operation of this system would engender its own subtle and effective civic virtue. See "New Readings of Tocqueville's *America*: Lessons for Democracy" in *Polity* 25:2 (1992): 282–99.

11. Even the limits on government are telling, since the most effective limit on government in the 1787 Constitution, the Federalists thought, was competition among officials in various branches of government. Federalists did not much trust the efficacy of the separation of powers so admired by Montesquieu and the Anti-Federalists, nor did they trust the efficacy of popular elections as a check on potential tyranny in the planned government. They placed their greatest trust in "ambition" counteracting ambition as the Constitution's greatest defense against tyranny.

12. The history of the gradual triumph of the Federalist conceptions of citizenship, democracy, and political party has not yet been written. Much of it is commonplace—like the still evident success of the Progressive movement (as distinct from the Populist movement) and the tacit but powerful influence that Social Darwinism still exercises on American politics. Authors like Wilson Carey McWilliams, Garry Wills, Theodore Lowi, and even (unknowingly perhaps) the venerable Louis Hartz have all contributed to this history.

13. Alexander Hamilton was especially concerned about such problems. See Federalist #6, #7, #9, and #17. A long history of such fears is evident in the unfolding of Federalist thought in American politics, from the Alien and Sedition Acts to current immigration policy debates.

14. See William N. Chambers' pathbreaking research on the historical and intellectual origin of political parties in the United States and the linkage between these political parties and the efficacy of democracy in the United States. See his: *Political Parties in a New Nation* (New York: Harper & Row, 1963); "Party Development and Party Action: The American Origins," *History and Theory* 3:1 (1963): 39–52; and, "Parties and Nation-Building in America," in J. LaPalombara and M. Weiner's *Political Parties and Political Development* (Princeton: Princeton University Press, 1966).

15. John White, one of the editors of this volume, has a wonderful and telling story to relate that illustrates this better than any statistic. While giving testimony on Capitol Hill about political parties, a Democratic member (let's keep him nameless) explained to John in some detail that parties mean nothing in today's politics, and that indeed they should mean nothing. The implication was that political parties were odious distortions in a democracy because "good politics" required that citizens participate on the basis of their own rationally considered self-interest.

16. James Ceaser. *Presidential Selection*. (Princeton: Princeton University Press, 1979). See especially his "Conclusion," 304–353.

17. James L. Sundquist. *Dynamics of the Party System*. (Washington: Brookings, 1973).

18. Kevin P. Phillips. *Post-Conservative America: People, Politics, and Ideology in a Time of Crisis*. (New York: Vintage, 1983), 233.

19. Robert Dahl. *Polyarchy.* (New Haven: Yale University Press, 1971).

20. Theodore Lowi. *The End of Liberalism.* (Ithaca, NY: Cornell University Press, 1973).

21. Impartial Examiner {Luther Martin?}. From Herbert Storing's *What the Anti-Federalists Were For* (Chicago: University of Chicago Press, 1981) 75.

22. Impartial Examiner, 75.

References

Abramson, Paul R., John H. Aldrich, and David W. Rohde. *Change and Continuity in the 1992 Elections*. Washington, DC: CQ Press, 1994.

Ackerman, Bruce. "The Broken Engine of Progressive Politics." *The American Prospect* 38. (May–June 1998): 34–43. <http://www.epn.org/prospect/ 38/38ackefs.html>.

Adams, Henry. *The Education of Henry Adams*. Boston: Houghton Mifflin, 1961.

Ambrose, Stephen E. *Eisenhower, Volume II, The President*. New York: Simon and Schuster, 1984.

American Political Science Association Committee on Political Parties. *Toward a More Responsible Two-Party System*. New York: Rinehart, 1950.

Arendt, Hannah. *Crises of the Republic*. New York: Harcourt Brace, 1969.

Aristotle. *Politics*. 1252b8–1253a3.

Associated Press. 1998. <www.daily.ou.edu/ideas/1998/november-03/ boston.html>.

Baker, Peter. "Judge Orders Lewinsky to Cooperate," *Washington Post*. 24 January 1999, A-18.

Balz, Dan. "Democrats Chart the Way Back," *Washington Post*. 19 November 1984, A1.

Barber, Benjamin R. *Jihad vs. McWorld: How Globalism and Tribalism Are Reshaping the World*. New York: Ballantine, 1996.

Barnes, James A. "Inside Bush's Campaign Shop." *National Journal*. August 1999, 2306–2307.

Bellah, Robert, et al. *Habits of the Heart*. Berkeley and Los Angeles: University of California Press, 1985.

Bennett, James and Pear, Robert. "Clinton's Little Initiatives Lead to Substantial Changes in Some Areas." *New York Times*, 8 December 1997, A1.

Bennett, W. Lance. "The Uncivil Culture: Communication, Identity and the Rise of Lifestyle Politics." *PS* 31 (1998): 750–753.

Berelson, Bernard, Paul F. Lazarsfeld, and William N. McPhee. *Voting*. Chicago: University of Chicago Press, 1954.

Berke, Richard L. "An Identity Crisis in the U.S." *New York Times*, 31 January 1999, WK1.

Berke, Richard L. with Janet Elder. "Damaged by Clinton Trial, Senate Sinks in Public's Eye; GOP is Hurt More." *New York Times*, 3 February 1999, A-1.

Blair, Tony. *New Britain: My Vision of a Young Country*. Boulder, Colorado: Westview Press, 1997.

Bluestone, Barry, and Stephen Rose. "Overworked and Underemployed." *American Prospect*, March/April 1997.

Boaz, David. *Libertarianism: A Primer*. New York: Free Press, 1997.

Bolick, Clinton. *Grassroots Tyranny: The Limits of Federalism*. Washington: Cato Institute, 1993.

Borosage, Robert L. "Look Who's Battling Global Capitalists." *Houston Chronicle*, 5 July 1998 Outlook, 1.

Boston Evening Globe. October 1928. "Boston Gives Heart to Smith: Greeting Breaks All Records," sec. 24, 1.

Bowles, Samuel, and Herbert Gintis. "Is Equality Passé?" *Boston Review* December 1998/January 1999, 4–7.

Brubaker, Stanley C. "Can Liberals Punish?" *American Political Science Review* 82 (1988): 821–836.

Brutus {Robert Yates?}. Letter I. *New York Journal*, 18 October 1787. From Allen, W. B. and Gordon Lloyd, eds. *The Essential Antifederalist*. Washington: UPA, 1985.

Burns, James MacGregor. *The Power to Lead*. New York: Simon and Schuster, 1984.

Ceaser, James. *Presidential Selection*. Princeton: Princeton University Press, 1979.

Ceaser, James and Andrew Busch. *Upside Down and Inside Out: The 1992 Elections and American Politics*. Lanham, Maryland: Rowman and Littlefield/Littlefield Adams Quality Paperbacks, 1993.

Chait, Jonathan. "The Slippery Center." *The New Republic*, 16 November 1998, 19.

Chambers, William N. "Party Development and Party Action: The American Origins." *History and Theory*. 3:1 (1963): 39–52.

Chambers, William N. *Political Parties in a New Nation*. New York: Harper & Row, 1963.

Clinton, Bill. "The New Covenant: Responsibility and Rebuilding the American Community." Address at Georgetown University. Washington, DC. 23 October 1991. In Robert E. Levin. *Bill Clinton: The Inside Story*. New York: S.P.I./Shapolsky, 1992.

Clinton, Bill and Al Gore. *Putting People First: How We All Can Change America*. New York: Times Books, 1992.

Cohen, Richard E. and James A. Barnes. "The Parties Adrift." *National Journal*, 25 April 1998, 918.

Cohen, Roger. "A Matter of Trust for Europe." *New York Times*, 31 January 1999, WK1.

Connelly, William F. Jr., and John J. Pitney, Jr. *Congress' Permanent Minority? Republicans in the US House*. Lanham, Maryland: Rowman and Littlefield, 1994.

Cook, Charles E. "GOP Can't Count on Clinton's Woes to Bring '94 Success." *Roll Call*, 10 May 1993, 9.

Cooper, Kenneth J. and Kevin Merida. "Republican Dilemma: To Defend the Past or Define the Future." *Washington Post*, 28 February 1993, A4.

Cronin, Thomas and Robert Loevy. "The Case for a National Pre-Primary Convention." *Public Opinion*, December/January 1983, 50–53.

Dahl, Robert. *Polyarchy*. New Haven: Yale University Press, 1971.

Daniel, Caroline. "Democrats Spend Week Giving Direction to 'Third Way' Ideology." *Washington Post*, 27 September 1998, A-28.

de Jouvenel, Bertrand. *Sovereignty*. Trans. J. F. Huntington. Indianapolis: Liberty Fund, 1997.

de Tocqueville, Alexis. *Democracy in America*. New York: Knopf, 1980.

Democratic National Committee. *The Democratic Party Platform*. Washington, DC: Democratic National Committee, 1992.

Dewey, John. *The Public and its Problems*. New York: Holt, 1927.

Dickenson, James R. "Democrats Seek Identity After Loss." *Washington Post*, 17 December 1984, A6.

Diggins, John P. *The Lost Soul of American Politics.* Chicago: University of Chicago Press, 1986.

Dionne, E. J., Jr. "Catholics and the Democratic Estrangement but not Desertion." Seymour Martin Lipset, ed. *Party Coalitions in the 1980s.* San Francisco: Institute for Contemporary Studies, 1981.

Dionne, E. J., Jr. "Construction Boon: It's No Accident That the GOP Is Being Rebuilt by Its Governors." *Washington Post,* 14 March 1999, B-4.

Dionne, E. J., Jr. *They Only Look Dead: Why Progressives Will Dominate the Next Political Era.* New York: Simon and Schuster, 1996.

Easterbrook, Gregg. "Ideas Move Nations." *Atlantic Monthly,* January 1986.

Edsall, Thomas B. "The Special Interest Gambit." *The Washington Post,* 3 January 1993, C1

Eldersveld, Samuel J. *Political Parties in American Society.* New York: Basic, 1982.

Ellul, Jacques. *The Technological Society.* New York: Vintage, 1964.

Elshtain, Jean Bethke. *Democracy on Trial.* New York: Basic Books, 1995.

Elving, Ronald D. *Conflict and Compromise: How Congress Makes the Law.* New York: Simon and Schuster, 1995.

Epstein, Leon D. *Political Parties in the American Mold.* Madison: University of Wisconsin Press, 1986.

Etzioni, Amitai. *The New Golden Rule: Community and Morality in Democratic Society.* New York: Basic Books, 1996.

Fiorina, Morris P. *Retrospective Voting in American National Elections.* New Haven: Yale University Press, 1981.

Forbes, Steve. Commencement address at Claremont McKenna College, Claremont, California, 18 May 1997 (privately printed).

Galston, William and Elaine Ciulla Kamarck. *The Politics of Evasion: Democrats and the Presidency.* Washington, DC: The Progressive Policy Institute, 1989.

Gates, Jeff. "The Ownership Solution." *Boston Review,* December 1998/January 1999, 32–33.

George Washington's Farewell Address. *Writings of George Washington.* New York: G.P. Putnam and Sons, 1889–93.

Gilens, Martin. *Why Americans Hate Welfare: Race, Media, and the Politics of Antipoverty Policy.* Chicago: University of Chicago Press, 1999.

Gimpel, James G. and James R. Edwards, Jr. *The Congressional Politics of Immigration Reform*. Needham Heights, Massachusetts: Allyn and Bacon, 1999.

Ginsberg, Benjamin, and Martin Shefter. *Politics By Other Means*. New York: Basic Books, 1990.

Gitlin, Todd. *The Twilight of Common Dreams*. New York: Henry Holt, 1995.

Glendon, Mary Ann. *Rights Talk: The Impoverishment of Political Discourse*. New York: Basic Books, 1991.

Goldman, Ralph M. "Who Speaks for the Political Parties or, Martin Van Buren, Where Are You When We Need You?" In *The State of the Parties*. John C. Green and Daniel M. Shea, eds. Lanham, Maryland: Rowman and Littlefield Publishers, 1996. 25–41.

Gottfried, Paul and Thomas Fleming. *The Conservative Movement*. Boston: Twayne, 1988.

Greenberg, Stanley B. *Middle Class Dreams: The Politics and Power of the New American Majority*. New York: Times Books, 1995.

Griffin, Laura. "New Charities Put Focus on Emergency Aid Agencies." *Dallas Morning News*, 27 November 1997, 1.

Grimsley, Kristin Downey. "Leaner and Definitely Meaner." *Washington Post National Weekly*, 20–27 July 1998, 21.

Gutmann, Amy and Dennis Thompson. *Democracy and Disagreement*. Cambridge: Harvard University Press, 1996.

Hager, George. "GOP Tax-Cutting Budget Plans Open Double-Barrel Hill Debate." *Washington Post*, 18 March 1999, A-4.

Hale, Jon F. "In Search of a Message: Democrats in the Post-Great Society Era." In *Politics, Professionalism and Power: Modern Party Organization and the Legacy of Ray C. Bliss*. Ed. John C. Green. Akron, Ohio: Ray C. Bliss Institute, 1994.

Hale, Jon F. "The Making of the New Democrats." *Political Science Quarterly* 110 (Summer 1995). <http://www.epn.org/psq/pshale.html>.

Hamilton, Alexander, James Madison, and John Jay. *The Federalist Papers*. New York: Mentor Books, 1961.

Hayek, Friedrich. "Why I am Not a Conservative." *The Constitution of Liberty*. South Bend: Gateway, 1972, 397–411.

Huntington, Samuel P. "Conservatism as an Ideology." *American Political Science Review* 51 (June 1957): 454–473.

Inglehart, Ronald. *Modernization and Postmodernization*. Princeton: Princeton University Press, 1997, 304–305, 311.

Isackson, Noah. "Demand Grows for Basic Needs." *Chicago Tribune,* 11 December 1997, 7.

Johnson, Paul. *A History of the American People*. New York: HarperCollins, 1997.

Kamarck, Elaine Ciulla. "Towards a New Paradigm." *The Mainstream Democrat,* September 1990, 22.

Kaus, Mickey. *The End of Equality*. New York: Basic Books, 1992.

Kaus, Mickey. "Paradigm's Loss." *The New Republic,* 27 July 1992, 18.

Kaus, Mickey. "They Blew It." *The New Republic,* 5 December 1994, 14–19.

Kesler, Charles R. "All American?" *National Review,* 7 December 1998, 52–55.

Key, V. O. *The Responsible Electorate: Rationality in Presidential Voting, 1936–1962*. New York: Vintage Books, 1966.

Kirk, Russell. *Beyond the Dreams of Avarice*. Chicago: Regnery, 1956.

Klinkner, Philip A. "Court and Country in American Politics: The Democratic Party in 1994." In *Midterm: The Elections of 1994*. Boulder, CO: Westview Press, 1996.

Klinkner, Philip A. *The Losing Parties: Out-Party National Committees, 1956–1993*. New Haven: Yale University Press, 1994.

Koch, Adrienne, and William Peden, eds. *Life and Selected Writings of Thomas Jefferson*. New York: Modern Library, 1944.

Kolodny, Robin. "The Contract with America in the 104th Congress." In *The State of the Parties*. 2d ed. Edited by John C. Green and Daniel M. Shea. Lanham, Maryland: Rowman and Littlefield, 1996.

Koopman, Douglas L. *Hostile Takeover: The House Republican Party 1980–1995*. Lanham, Maryland: Rowman and Littlefield, 1996.

Ladd, Everett Carll. "Like Waiting for Godot: The Uselessness of Realignment of Understanding Change in Contemporary American Politics." *Polity* (Spring 1990): 511–525.

Ladd, Everett Carll. *Where Have All the Voters Gone?* Rev. ed. New York: W.W. Norton, 1982.

Landy, Marc K., and Martin A. Levin, eds. *The New Politics of Public Policy*. Baltimore: Johns Hopkins University Press, 1995.

Lardner, James. "Ask Radio Historians About the Internet." *U.S. News and World Report*, 25 January 1999, 48.

Leach, James and William P. McKenzie, eds. *A Newer World: The Progressive Republican Vision of America*. Lanham, Maryland: Madison Books, 1989.

Lewis, C. S. *Mere Christianity*. New York: Macmillan, Collier Books, 1952.

Lewis-Beck, Michael S. and Tom W. Rice. *Forecasting Elections*. Washington, DC: CQ Press, 1992.

Lipovetsky, Gilles. "May '68, or the Rise of Transpolitical Individualism." Trans. L. Maguire. In *New French Thought*, ed. Mark Lilla, Princeton: Princeton University Press, 1994.

Lippmann, Walter. *The Phantom Public*. New York: Macmillan, 1925.

Locke, John. *A Letter Concerning Toleration*. Indianapolis: Bobbs Merrill, 1955.

Locke, John. *The Reasonableness of Christianity*. Edited by I. T, Ramsey. Stanford: Stanford University Press, 1958.

Lowi, Theodore. *The End of Liberalism*. Ithaca, NY: Cornell University Press, 1973.

Lowi, Theodore J. "Think Globally, Lose Locally." *Boston Review*, April/May 1998, 4–10.

Lowi, Theodore J. "Toward a Responsible Three-Party System." In Theodore J. Lowi and Joseph Romance, *A Republic of Parties: Debating the Two-Party System*. Lanham: Rowman and Littlefield, 1998.

Mansfield, Harvey. *America's Constitutional Soul*. Baltimore: Johns Hopkins University Press, 1991.

Maraniss, David. *First in His Class*. New York: Simon and Schuster, 1995.

Marx and Engels. *The Communist Manifesto*. London: Penguin, 1985.

Mayhew, David R. "The Return to Unified Party Control Under Clinton: How Much of a Difference in Lawmaking?" In Bryan D. Jones, editor. *The New American Politics: Reflections on Political Change and the Clinton Administration*. Boulder, CO: Westview Press, 1995.

McGovern, George. *Grassroots: The Autobiography of George McGovern*. New York: Random House, 1977.

McGurn, William. "Abortion and the GOP." *National Review*, 15 March 1993, 52.

McWilliams, Wilson Carey. "Democracy and the Citizen: Community Dignity, and the Crisis of Contemporary Politics in America." *How Democratic is the Constitution?* Edited by Robert A. Goldwin and William A. Schambra. Washington, DC: AEI, 1980.

McWilliams, Wilson C. "In Good Faith: On the Foundations of American Politics." *Humanities in Society* 6 (1983): 32–35.

Mileur, Jerome M. "Massachusetts: The Democratic Party Charter Movement." In *Party Renewal in America*, edited by Gerald M. Pomper. New York: Praeger, 1980.

Miller, Merle. *Lyndon: An Oral Biography.* New York: Ballantine Books, 1980.

Morris, Dick. *Behind the Oval Office: Winning the Presidency in the Nineties.* New York: Random House, 1997.

Moynihan, Daniel Patrick. *The Politics of a Guaranteed Income: The Administration and the Family Assistance Plan.* New York: Random House, Vintage Books, 1973.

Nash, George H. *The Conservative Intellectual Movement in America since 1945.* New York: Basic Books, 1976.

"New Readings of Tocqueville's *America*: Lessons for Democracy" *Polity* 25:2 (1992): 282–99.

Nixon, Richard M. *Beyond Peace.* New York: Random House, 1994.

O'Brien, Dennis. "City's 30 Shelters Filled to Capacity." *Baltimore Sun,* 5 December 1997, 1B.

Ostrogorski, M. *Democracy and the Organization of Political Parties.* New York: Reeve's, 1902.

"Parties and Nation-Building in America." In J. LaPalombara and M. Weiner *Political Parties and Political Development.* Princeton: Princeton University Press, 1966.

Phelps, Edmund. *Reworking Work.* Cambridge: Harvard University Press, 1997.

Phillips, Kevin P. *Post-Conservative America: People, Politics, and Ideology in a Time of Crisis.* New York: Vintage, 1983.

Pinkerton, James P. "Reagan's Legacy — Unbridled Capitalism." *Newsday,* 1 February 1996, A43.

Pinkerton, James P. *What Comes Next: The End of Big Government and the New Paradigm Ahead.* New York: Hyperion, 1995.

Pitney, John J., Jr. "Republican Alternatives to the Great Society." In *Politics, Professionalism and Power: Modern Party Organization and the Legacy of*

Ray C. Bliss. Edited by John C. Green. Akron, Ohio: Ray C. Bliss Institute, 1994.

Pitney, John J., Jr. "Tangled Web." *Reason,* April 1996, 52.

Podhoretz, John. *Hell of a Ride: Backstage at the White House Follies.* New York: Simon and Schuster, 1993.

Polanyi, Karl. *The Great Transformation.* Boston: Beacon, 1957.

Pomper, Gerald M. "Primaries *After* Conventions." *New York Times,* 2 January 1998, 23.

Pool, Ithiel deSola. *Technologies without Boundaries.* Cambridge: Harvard University Press, 1990.

Postrel, Virginia. *The Future and Its Enemies: The Growing Conflict Over Creativity, Enterprise, and Progress.* New York: Free Press, 1998.

Price, David E. *Bringing Back the Parties.* Washington, DC: Congressional Quarterly, 1984.

Putnam, Robert. "Bowling Alone: America's Declining Social Capital." *Journal of Democracy* 6 (1995): 65–78.

Quirk, Paul J. and Jon K. Dalager. "The Election: A 'New Democrat' and a New Kind of Presidential Campaign." In *The Elections of 1992.* Edited by Michael Nelson. Washington, DC: Congressional Quarterly Press, 1993.

Rae, Nicol C. *The Decline and Fall of the Liberal Republicans from 1952 to the Present.* New York: Oxford University Press, 1989.

Reichley, A. James. "Republican Ideology and the American Future." In *The Politics of Ideas: Intellectual Challenges to the Major Parties After 1992.* Edited by John K. White and John C. Green. Lanham, Maryland: Rowman and Littlefield, 1995.

Robertson, Pat. *The New World Order.* Dallas: Word, 1991.

Rose, Gary L., ed. *Controversial Issues in Presidential Selection.* Albany: State University of New York Press, 1991.

Rosenblum, Nancy. *Membership and Morals: The Personal Uses of Pluralism in America.* Princeton: Princeton University Press, 1998.

Rosenstiel, Tom. *Strange Bedfellows: How Television and the Presidential Candidates Changed American Politics, 1992.* New York: Hyperion, 1994.

Rosenstone, Steven J. *Forecasting Presidential Elections.* New Haven: Yale University Press, 1983.

Saad, Lydia. "GOP Image Losing Its Luster." *The Polling Report,* 30 November 1998, 1.

Sandel, Michael. "America's Search for a New Public Philosophy." *Atlantic Monthly*, March 1996, 58.

Sandel, Michael. *Democracy's Discontents: America in Search of a Public Philosophy*. Cambridge: Harvard University Press, 1996.

Sartori, Giovanni. *Parties and Party System: A Framework for Analysis*. Cambridge, Massachusetts: Harvard University Press, 1976.

Schattschneider, E. E. *Party Government*. New York: Rinehart, 1942.

Schattschneider, E. E. *The Struggle for Party Government*. College Park, Maryland: Program in American Civilization, University of Maryland, 1948.

Schlesinger, Arthur M., Jr. *The Vital Center*. Boston: Houghton Mifflin, 1949.

Schneider, William. "No Modesty Please, We're the DLC." *National Journal*, 12 December 1998.

Shalit, Ruth. "What I Saw at the Devolution." *Reason*, March 1993, 27.

Shields, Mark. "California's Comeback Kid." *Washington Post*, 22 March 1998, C-11.

Sidey, Hugh. "A Conversation with Reagan." *Time*, 3 September 1984.

Skowronek, Stephen. *The Politics Presidents Make: Leadership from John Adams to George Bush*. Cambridge, Massachusetts: Harvard University Press/Belknap, 1993.

Skowronek, Stephen. "The Risks of 'Third-Way' Politics," *Society*, September/October 1996, 32–36.

Small, Melvin. *The Presidency of Richard Nixon*. Lawrence, Kansas: University Press of Kansas, 1999.

Smith, Alfred E. *Up to Now: An Autobiography*. New York: Viking Press, 1929.

Smith, Rogers. *Civic Ideals*. New Haven: Yale University Press, 1997.

Stanley, Harold W. and Richard G. Niemi. *Vital Statistics on American Politics*. Washington, DC: Congressional Quarterly Press, 1990.

Stanley, Harold W. and Richard G. Niemi. *Vital Statistics on American Politics, Fourth Edition*. Washington, DC: CQ Press, 1994.

Stanley, Harold W. and Richard G. Niemi. *Vital Statistics on American Politics 1997–1998*. Washington, DC: Congressional Quarterly Press, 1998.

Stone, Peter H. "Family Feud." *National Journal* 30 (2 May 1998): 987.

Storing, Herbert. *What the Anti-Federalists Were For*. Chicago: University of Chicago Press, 1981.

Strout, Richard L. "Restoring America's Parties." *Christian Science Monitor*, 25 September 1977, 31.

Sundquist, James L. *Dynamics of the Party System*. Washington: Brookings, 1973.

Sundquist, James L. *Dynamics of the Party System: Alignment and Realignment of Political Parties in the United States*, Rev. ed. Washington, DC: Brookings Institution, 1983.

Teixeira, Ruy A. and Joel Rogers. "Who Deserted the Democrats in 1994?" *The American Prospect* 23 (Fall 1995): 73–36. <http://www.epn.org/prospect/23/23teix.html>.

Toffler, Alvin. "The *Playboy* Interview with Ayn Rand." In *The Libertarian Reader*, edited by David Boaz. New York: Free Press, 1997.

Toffler, Alvin. *PowerShift*. New York: Bantam, 1990.

Turow, Scott. "The Supreme Court's Twenty-Year-Old Mistake." *New York Times*, 12 October 1997, WK15.

"Voter Turnout Falls Sharply Among the Less Affluent." *The New York Times*, 11 June 1995, A16.

Waldman, Steven. *The Bill: How the Adventures of Clinton's National Service Bill Reveal What Is Corrupt, Comic, Cynical—and Noble—About Washington*. New York: Viking, 1995.

Wattenberg, Martin P. *The Rise of Candidate-Centered Politics*. Cambridge, Massachusetts: Harvard University Press, 1991.

Wattenberg, Martin P. "When You Can't Beat Them, Join Them: Shaping the Presidential Nominating Process to the Television Age." *Polity*, Summer 1989.

White, John Kenneth. *The New Politics of Old Values*. Hanover, New Hampshire: University Press of New England, 1988.

White, John Kenneth. *Still Seeing Red: How the Cold War Shapes the New American Politics*. Boulder, Colorado: Westview Press, 1998.

Wiebe, Robert. *The Search for Order, 1877–1920*. New York: Hill and Wang, 1966.

Wilcox, Clyde. *The Latest American Revolution?: The 1994 Elections and Their Implications for Governance*. New York: St. Martin's Press, 1995.

Wolfe, Alan. *One Nation After All*. New York: Viking, 1998.

Woodward, Bob. *The Agenda: Inside the Clinton White House*. New York: Simon and Schuster, 1994.

Woodward, Bob, and Peter Baker. "Behind Calm Air, President Hides Rage Over Starr." *Washington Post*, 1 March 1988, A-1.

Young, Iris Marion. *Justice and the Politics of Difference*. Princeton: Princeton University Press, 1990.

Young James C. *The Washington Community, 1800–1828*. New York: Columbia University Press, 1986.

Zaller, John. "Monica Lewinsky's Contribution to Political Science." *PS* 31 (1998): 182–189.

Contributors

JOHN C. GREEN is professor of political science and the director of the Ray C. Bliss Institute of Applied Politics at the University of Akron. He is the co-editor of *The State of the Parties: The Changing Role of Contemporary Party Politics,* soon to be in its fourth edition, and editor of *Financing the 1996 Election.* He is co-author of *The Diminishing Divide: Religion's Changing Role in Contemporary Politics* and *The Bully Pulpit: The Politics of Protestant Clergy.*

PHILIP KLINKNER is associate professor of government and director of the Arthur Levitt Public Affairs Center at Hamilton College in Clinton, New York. He is the author of *The Losing Parties: Out-Party National Committees, 1956–1993* and *The Unsteady March: The Rise and Decline of Racial Equality in America.* In 1995, he received the Emerging Scholar Award from the Political Organizations and Parties section of the American Political Science Association.

EVERETT CARLL LADD was executive director and president of the Roper Center for Public Opinion Research at the University of Connecticut and an adjunct scholar of the American Enterprise Institute in Washington, DC. Dr. Ladd authored or edited twenty books on American political thought, electoral politics, and public opinion. His last book was titled *The Ladd Report.* It described how an explosion of voluntary groups, activities, and charitable donations is transforming American towns and cities. Dr. Ladd died in December 1999.

WILSON CAREY MCWILLIAMS is professor of political science at Rutgers University. He is the author of *Beyond the Politics of Disappointment?*

167

and *The Idea of Fraternity in America*, which won the National Historical Society Prize in 1973. He is a frequent contributor to
Commonweal and other journals of opinion.

JOHN J. PITNEY JR. is associate professor of government at Claremont
McKenna College, in Claremont, California. A former congressional
fellow of the American Political Science Association, he has written a
number of works on Congress, the presidency, and campaign politics.
He is the author of *The Art of Political Warfare*, published in 2000
by the University of Oklahoma Press.

STEPHEN F. SCHNECK is an associate professor at The Catholic
University of America. He writes and teaches in the field of political
theory with a particular emphasis on 20ᵗʰ century and American political thought.

JOHN KENNETH WHITE is professor of politics at the Catholic
University of America. His previous books include *New Party Politics:
From Hamilton and Jefferson to the Information Age* (coauthored with
Daniel M. Shea); *Political Parties and the Collapse of the Old Orders*
(edited with Philip J. Davies); *Still Seeing Red: How the Cold War
Shapes the New American Politics*; *Challenges to Party Government*
(edited with Jerome M. Mileur); *The New Politics of Old Values*; and
*The Fractured Electorate: Political Parties and Social Change in South-
ern New England*.

Index